FIDES SPES CARITAS

MOUNT SACKVILLE

1864 - 2004

by
Mary Delaney

Published by

Sisters of St. Joseph of Cluny

Mount Sackville
Chapelizod
Dublin 20

ISBN No: 0-9549652-0-5

ISBN 0-9549652-0-5

9 780954 965204

Printed by JETPRINT
Tullamore, Co. Offaly.
Tel: 0506 - 41373

*This book is a tribute to
Mother Callixte Pichet
who founded Mount Sackville in 1864
and to the many sisters and teachers who have worked
in the school for the past one hundred and forty years.*

Our thanks to our sponsors

Bank of Scotland (Ireland) Ltd
Anglo Irish Bank

Contents

Preface

In a letter written by Mother Callixte Pichet to her superior in France in June 1864, Mount Sackville is described as:

"Heaven on earth - in this world's language
it does express the beauty of the place."

Mount Sackville Secondary School was founded in 1864 by the sisters of Saint Joseph of Cluny. The school is idyllically situated above the valley of the River Liffey, between Castleknock and Chapelizod and adjoins the Phoenix Park.

Since its foundation, it has taken its place among the leading secondary schools in Ireland and has been synonymous with the education of young women for the last 140 years. It encourages the pursuit of excellence, while offering a high standard of teaching and learning opportunities.

Today the school accommodates over six hundred and thirty day pupils drawn from its urban and rural hinterlands and comprises a teaching staff of over fifty highly-qualified, experienced and enthusiastic teachers.

As a member of the teaching staff for the last twelve years, I feel honoured to have been asked to compile a brief history of the school since its foundation in 1864. As it would be impossible to deal with all 140 years in great detail, I hope that this booklet, outlining the origin and growth of the school, will be of interest to pupils both past and present and to the many people associated with Mount Sackville.

Mary Delaney, Editor

Acknowledgements

I would like to thank the following:

Sister Maeve Guinan, Provincial of the Sisters of St Joseph of Cluny for her encouragement and guidance.

Mrs. Marian McCaughley, School Principal for her advice and support.

Sister Enda Hanley, Archivist in Mount Sackville, for her help in researching this history.

The many past pupils who submitted memoirs and photographs.

My colleagues on the teaching staff, Trish Lanigan of the Art Department, Mary Begley, Peter Burke and Gerard Murphy. Bernadette Buckley, Margaret Boylan and Carol Kearney of the secretarial staff and also Mary McHugh, former English teacher in Mount Sackville for her invaluable help.

Those Transition Year Students, who enthusiastically helped to carry out interviews, collect photographs and research exam results.

The staff of the National Archives, Bishop's Street, Dublin, the Ordnance Survey Office of Ireland, Phoenix Park and to Mr. Jim Lacey, local historian, for materials used in the text.

Mrs. Tracey Crampton for typing the booklet and to Lorraine and all the staff at Jetprint, Tullamore, Co. Offaly for their help in the production of this publication.

Mary Delaney, Editor

Introduction

Sister Maeve Guinan

We welcome the publication of this short history of Mount Sackville School which coincides with the 140th Anniversary of its foundation.

We are deeply grateful to Mary Delaney, Head of the History Department in Mount Sackville, for undertaking to research and write this story. Her love for the school and her skill and experience as a local historian make her superbly qualified for the task.

Mount Sackville has evolved from being a handful of students in 1864 to a thriving modern school of over six hundred and thirty girls today. Mary has faithfully chronicled this development and shown how despite this growth, the school has retained its warm, family atmosphere, where each student feels valued as a person and receives limitless encouragement to develop all facets of her personality and her talents. The school has preserved and enhanced its strong tradition of Music, Art and languages and its awareness of and care for those less fortunate. Anne Marie Javouhey's dictum to *"love the children"* and to *"make a great effort to improve the education and raise it to as high a degree of perfection as possible"* has had a central place in the philosophy of Mount Sackville. Girls educated in Mount Sackville have founded schools stamped with this characteristic spirit in the far flung corners of the five continents.

We are grateful to the Principals and Staff who, down through the years, gave of themselves so generously to the task of educating our youth and we are pleased to know that Mrs. McCaughley and her Staff continue to enhance the proud tradition of Mount Sackville in every possible way. With total confidence we welcome the next page in the history of Mount Sackville.

Sister Maeve Guinan
Provincial of the Sisters of Saint Joseph of Cluny

A message from our Principal

Principal, Mrs. Marian McCaughley

Mount Sackville in 2004 enjoys the same beautiful location chosen by Sr. Callixte Pichet in 1864 and the school today continues the work of education begun by the Cluny sisters in the nineteenth century.

Today the school no longer has boarders, but instead has six hundred and thirty day students drawn mostly from counties Dublin, Meath and Kildare. The programme of education followed is a six-year cycle which includes a valuable transition year. Many of our current students come from families where mothers, fathers, grandparents and other members have happy memories of attending school in Mount Sackville. Our staff also has a rich representation of past pupils who continue the development of the educational traditions they experienced here themselves as students.

The original curriculum offered in Mount Sackville was very limited by today's standards. It included Art, Music, Needlework, Literature, French and Mathematics. In response to changes in society and the developing role of women there has been a major expansion in the curriculum over the decades. Opportunities were limited for those girls who completed their education here in the 1860's. Running a house, marriage, nursing, teaching or entering the Cluny order were the alternatives of the day. Many young women entered the novitiate from Mount Sackville and went to work on the missions as Cluny sisters and opened schools and hospitals across the globe wherever the need was the greatest.

The Cluny commitment to the pursuit of excellence is evident today in students' achievements in many areas of school life such as their Junior and Leaving Certificate examinations, in Sport, in Art and in Music. The curriculum is based on the study of the core subjects of Irish, English, Mathematics and Religion. It has expanded to include the Sciences and Home Economics. Biology, Physics and Chemistry, contrary to national trends at present, are popular at Leaving Certificate level where students achieve high standards. Business subjects include Accounting, Business and Economics and the languages offered comprise French, German and Italian. The Humanities include History, Geography, Classical Studies, Art and Music. Physical Education and team sports are part of the curriculum at all levels and get special mention by pupils as some of the most popular activities of school life.

Students go on to further study in all these areas and Mount Sackville students are represented in the different faculties at University and College and in the professions.

Today's students also interpret the advice of the foundress, Blessed Anne-Marie Javouhey to *"do a little good"* by their involvement in supporting local and mission needs through a number of active charities in the school. These vary from the work of the Saint Vincent de Paul conference to "Focus on Romania" campaigning for improvements in Romanian Orphanages and also through visiting the sick and elderly as part of their community work programme. Prayer and reflection are an integral part of school life, through the celebration of the sacraments, of the liturgical seasons and the retreat programme of the school.

The challenges facing education in Ireland today are considerably different from those of the 1860's and in more recent times the changing nature of the family and the increase in disposable income place greater demands on young people in every area of their lives. The urge to seek our own pleasure and to remain isolated in comfort while ignoring the needs of others in our own communities and in the world community has become a feature of modern life. This has happened just as Ireland joined the ranks of the wealthiest countries in the world and yet we have seen an increase in poverty over the same period.

The isolation we feel when living in a self-centred way, brings no happiness or joy to the human spirit. The true happiness we all seek lies in making a difference in some way to the lives of others and our students are very open to the search for justice in the world in their efforts to meet the needs of others. This spirit is alive and well in the school today.

> *"Ours is not to reap the harvest, ours is just to sow the seed"*
> Blessed Anne-Marie Javouhey.

The involvement of parents in the school has been formalised in recent years. In a spirit of partnership the first Board of Management was set up in 1998. In the following years the school has undertaken a programme of developing new facilities and of improving the learning opportunities for all students with parents' support. The leadership, wisdom, strength and skill of the Boards of Management have energised the school for the benefit of all.

The tradition of parental participation in school life is not a recent one in Mount Sackville. It is epitomised by the valuable work of the Parents' Association over the generations, tirelessly supporting the work of the school and facilitating communication between school and home, providing lectures and support for parents and running events for parents and students. The work of the staff is supported by the interest of parents in their daughters' welfare and concern for their development. In their turn the students are consulted on issues concerning the running of the school through their representative body, the Student Forum.

We were honoured by a visit from President Mary McAleese in May 2004 to commemorate the 140th anniversary. She reminded us of an old Chinese proverb:

> *" Those who drink from the well should thank those who dug the well"*

Today we pause to reflect on the history of the school and to appreciate the gift given to the present generation by those who began the "digging of the well" of faith and learning in Mount Sackville 140 years ago. We thank all the sisters, teachers, parents and friends who contributed to the development of the school over that time, Ms. Mary Delaney for her tireless work in researching this history and all those who assisted by contributing materials.

Marian McCaughley, Principal

The Foundation of the order of Saint Joseph of Cluny

Blessed Anne-Marie Javouhey

The order of the sisters of Saint Joseph of Cluny was founded in 1807 by blessed Anne-Marie Javouhey. She was a remarkable woman with ideas well ahead of her time. All through her life, she lived her faith through concrete actions focussed on the needs of people around her. These actions centred on three main areas:-

> • her devotion to helping people who were suffering - either
> through sickness or poverty;

- looking after the educational needs of children;
- her strong desire to help peoples of all races and in particular, to fight the evil of slavery.

All of these became central themes in the work of the St. Joseph of Cluny Sisters. Indeed, these themes are very much at the heart of the work of the Order in today's world. There are modern forms of slavery which are just as damaging as the original form. Marginalisation, poverty, drugs, prostitution, promiscuity, violence and the frantic pursuit of wealth are just some of the modern forms of slavery that ruin the lives of many people. And wherever Anne-Marie Javouhey's Cluny Order is working in today's world they continue to fight each of these modern scourges that prevent people from reaching their full potential as children of God.

The farm in Jallanges where Anne-Marie Javouhey was born

A Brief Biography

Anne-Marie Javouhey was born in the modest village of Jallanges in the Dijon area of eastern France. From these humble beginnings, she would eventually travel to many remote and dangerous parts of the world - in an era when the majority of people never travelled much further than to their neighbouring town during their whole lives. Anne-Marie Javouhey was a woman with a strong mission from God and her inspirational, crusading spirit led her to found a religious Order that still works and thrives in the world of the 21st century. She was genuinely a woman ahead of her time. Pope Pius IX referred to her as *"the first woman missionary"*; Louis-Philippe of France described her as a *"great man"* - an epithet with which today's feminists might well want to quarrel, but taking the comment in the context of the 19th century, it is undoubtedly an accolade of the highest order.

Anne-Marie Javouhey was born in 1779, to the family of the local mayor - Balthazar Javouhey - and was baptised as Anne, the 'Marie' was added later as a mark of her devotion to the Blessed Virgin. Within the family she was known as Nannette.

The Javouhey home, Chamblanc

Anne-Marie was nine years old when the Paris mob stormed the Bastille, and she was barely fourteen when the French royal family were beheaded by revolutionaries.

It is part of Anne-Marie's legend that despite her youth she helped the priests who had been outlawed after the Civil Constitution of the Clergy was passed

- the infamous law that required the clergy to swear an oath of allegiance to the secular state, and made criminals of those who refused to take the oath. The helping of those priests was perhaps Anne-Marie's first real crusade.

At the same time she saw the importance of education for children. She gathered together and helped prepare the local children to receive the sacraments. She had a dream in which St. Teresa of Avila showed her children of different races whom God wished to confide to Anne-Marie's care. It was a dream that stayed with Anne-Marie throughout all the years. Children - the care and educating of them - was to be a recurring thread throughout her life.

Her family strongly supported her first endeavours with local children. There is a story of how her father arranged for her to borrow the village drum so that she could summon the children to her classes for religious instruction. No matter how she called them, they came to her. By this time, she was already quite aware of her own vocation.

In later years she wrote, *"I still see the place where I was ploughing when God made known His Will to me..."* But if she was sure, her father had doubts. He apparently thought Anne-Marie was *"too mischievous"* to receive her First Communion at the age of nine and worried that she might be *"too unstable"* to undertake the religious life at nineteen when she consecrated her life to God, in secret as public worship was still banned in France. So Anne-Marie waited, believing that *"God has His designs, He will make them known in time...He is in no hurry...."* In 1802 she wrote to her father, *"All your refusals will not discourage me... I think my heart would have to be snatched out to take away my desire for the religious life.."*

But Balthazar did not remain implacable; indeed, he was later to be of the greatest help to Anne-Marie, and the waiting time was valuable to her as a period of learning and gaining experience. Anne-Marie, exploring possibilities in these early years, tried a number of different paths upon which to follow what she believed was God's will for her. For a time she lived with a Trappist Order in Switzerland, and also in Besançon, in southern France. During this time Anne-Marie gradually became convinced that her true vocation lay in the founding of a completely new religious Order. By any standards this would have been an awesome undertaking, but to a girl still only in her twenties, the difficulties must have seemed in surmountable.

Or did they? By 1806, in the town of Chalon, she had succeeded in establishing an Institute, which she dedicated to St. Joseph. Her father gave her immense practical support, buying rooms and houses in which she could work towards her dream of educating children and orphans.

One of the buildings he bought was in Cluny - the former Recollects Convent, and a few years after its purchase, the church and state both gave recognition to the small congregation of nine nuns, three of whom were Anne-Marie's own sisters. The Order was henceforth officially known as the Sisters of St. Joseph of Cluny. And so a piece of history was made.

Now Anne-Marie's work could really begin, and as the numbers of the Convent increased, the never-forgotten dream of St. Teresa of Avila and the children began to take on real substance.

There were years of expansion and progress. More novices joined Anne-Marie, and a Paris House was founded - the *'School of the Marsh'*. The course should have seemed set fair, so much had been destroyed by the Revolution whole communities had been lost; *"Everything seems to make this project impossible..."* she wrote.

The Paris project was an immense struggle, there was no money, and no resources of any kind. It was necessary to draw water from the Seine in order to drink and wash, and food came mostly from leftovers in the markets, although once again Balthazar Javouhey helped, sending cartloads of food for the small community.

Anne-Marie began her school for the poor, and in time she became noticed. In 1814 she was asked to work in the French Colonies to help with the organising of schools and hospitals. It was work dear to her heart and she accepted. So from those early struggles came the beginnings of her real mission - in 1817 five sisters left for their long sea-voyage to Reunion.

Even to read the list of the places visited is striking. They went to the island of Reunion, near Madagascar, then known as Bourbon, but this was to be followed by Guadeloupe, Martinique, St. Pierre et Miquelon, Pondichery, Madagascar itself, and Mayotte. *"The perils of the sea do not frighten us,"* she wrote. *"Our aim is the hope of doing good, of winning a few souls for religion, of alleviating the poor sick and sustaining their courage in the midst of the greatest dangers...."*

In 1822 she travelled to Sengal and Sierra Leone in Africa. Anne-Marie had to contend with poverty, ignorance, disease and cruelty and the prejudice of many of the slave owners. Despite it, she took Africa to her heart and was fired with fresh zeal to help its people and improve their lives. She was way ahead of her time, she spoke out for the eminent dignity of all human beings and she preached fervently for equality at a time when the idea of equality for all races, colours and creeds was scarcely understood.

At her Beatification almost one hundred years after her death, Monsigneur Chappoulie, Bishop of Angers said of the journey she made to Senegal: *"Between the Mother Foundress of the Sisters of Cluny and the negro people there was at once sealed an alliance which will draw force from the supernatural love which this great soul, entirely given to Jesus Christ, bore to this disinherited race.."*?

By now she was truly an extraordinary woman. She had travelled to many countries in an era when travel was difficult and women were either regarded as the property of men, or were pampered and protected to an impossible degree.

In 1828 when she passed through Alençon on her way to Brest, she described: *"We came across an asylum that had eighty mentally ill of both sexes, and forty to fifty other sick people or unfortunates....There were at least thirty five dangerous people that could only be approached with armed security. Several of them were naked. Within three days we have managed to clothe, change and pacify them..."* Later the Sisters became known as the 'blue angels' to the inmates of the mental asylum in Alençon.

In Guyana, a short while afterwards, she reacted in much the same way when she saw lepers living on the island of Salut - existing without water or shade, exposed to the sea air that burned their wounds. For three years she bombarded the government to transfer them to a more comfortable place, and in the end she got her way. Again, her words paint the picture: *"It is a kind of hospital for 150 people, which will be about five leagues from Mana, in a nice location. We will be in charge of it.... My sisters rival with each other to have the honour of doing this hard work...."*

Hard work was something about which she knew and from which she never flinched. The work for lepers which she began continues within the Order to this day.

In her beloved Africa Anne-Marie had already made a start on helping to educate the slaves towards self-sufficiency, arranging for them to travel to France for training, and then back to their homeland. For a time there was a junior seminary in Senegal, although it closed after a tuberculosis outbreak. In 1840, she heard with delight, of the ordaining of three young Senegalese - the promotion of native clergy had always been a particular dream of hers.

In 1831, the French Government passed the bill for the abolition of the slave trade in all of the French colonies, and in 1835 the Ministers of Louis-Philippe asked Anne-Marie to take over 500 slaves from Guyana, and prepare them to make good use of their liberty. It was a task that Anne-Marie accepted eagerly.

She formed the idea of creating a village for them: the government had provided land on the banks of the Mana River, and Anne-Marie would train the liberated slaves, enabling them to understand the concept of earning their own living. Later, she wanted them to be given a little land of their own.

The Mana project was worthy and inspired, a portion of one of Anne-Marie's letters describes their progress in the village very vividly: *"We brought with us fifteen well chosen workmen...I visited their workshops at least four times a day, starting with the cabinet makers and carpenters, then into the turners..., the shoe makers.., the sawmills, forge, boiler-makers, mechanics.. When I have finished, I come back by the cultivators: first of all I visit the gardeners, then the men working on the land, after which I go to take a rest near the Sisters, whose work is quite equal to that of the men. It is in the company of these good Sisters that I weed, plant beans and manioc, sow rice and maize, while singing hymns and telling stories, and regretting that our poor Sisters in France cannot share our happiness.... Our solitude is watered by two beautiful navigable rivers full of fish; every day we eat more or less fish according to the skill of the fishermen; it costs us nothing and is a great economy for the kitchen..."*

It is, however, one of the ironies of her life that it was her work in Mana that brought to a head the simmering animosity directed against her, and plunged her into a period of darkness.

Ever since her inauguration as Mother Superior of the Order in 1835, there had been hostility from the Bishop of Autun, and in addition, there were men in high places who still had the 'colonial' mentality towards slaves - *"The safety of the white population rests on keeping the negroes in ignorance, and on treating them like beasts....It is not slavery that has made these races lazy: it is their laziness that has led them into slavery.."* She had to fight this attitude and on one occasion she had to cope with a more sinister hostility. The resentful slave-owners had hatched a plan to stage a river-boat accident, in order to rid themselves of the troublesome French nun who seemed set on disrupting their lives. Such an act would be outright murder, but murder well disguised and they must have thought there was a fair chance of success. However the details leaked out - perhaps Anne-Marie had more supporters and friends than the slave-owners had bargained for - and information about the plot was carried to her. Would she alter her plans and journey and so foil the plot? she was asked. She would not. She went ahead with the journey as it had been planned.

Even in today's modern world, it is easy enough to imagine that journey and all the sights and sounds of nineteenth-century Guyana, South America, that must have accompanied the travellers...Anne-Marie's companions anxiously watched the banks for enemies as they went along...but Anne-Marie herself seems not to have faltered. She trusted to God to protect her and she reached her destination unscathed.

The harm she did suffer at that time was of a different kind. Out of the plots and counter-plots that surrounded her came the decree of the Prefect Apostolic of Cayenne that she should be forbidden the sacraments. It was a ban that was to last for twenty months, and they must have been long and wearisome months for her. Perhaps, during that time, she clung to the glowing Old Testament promise of *"A lamp unto my feet and a light unto my path..."* The lamp illuminating her path burned steadily throughout.

What she referred to as her 'quasi-excommunication' was at last brought to an end by the intervention of Pope Gregory XVI, who issued an appeal to the Christian world to finish, once and for all, the appalling trafficking of human lives and end slavery. In 1845 the Bishop of Beauvais gave Anne-Marie his support, and in 1849 the Archbishop of Paris authorised the establishment of the principal novitiate at the Mother House in Paris.

Anne-Marie Javouhey was 64 when she returned to France; even so, there were still achievements to delight her - such as the receiving of a former West Indian slave girl into the congregation. That long ago dream of St. Teresa of Avila was far more than just a dream now.

Always ahead of her time, she had constantly shown interests in the beliefs and the ways of people from other religions. On meeting some people of the Muslim faith, she expressed admiration for their piety and talked to them about their religion. It is impossible not to think with what pleasure she would have welcomed Vatican II and the blurring of the religious divisions and with that delight she would have recognised the crucible into which the world's colours and races are today gradually being brought together. She would have recognised the setbacks and the difficulties as well, for setbacks and difficulties had been part of her whole life.

She was 71 when she died, and by then there were 1,200 Sisters of the Order, working in Africa, Asia, Australia, South America, Oceania and the West Indies. Her travels had been long and arduous and often dangerous, and her life had been filled with the most extraordinary adventures and achievements. Throughout it, she had been a crusader for the rights of humanity, and for the equality of all races and creeds - a freedom fighter before ever the phrase was coined. She has left behind a remarkable legacy to the Sisters of St. Joseph of Cluny who, with over 400 Houses throughout the world today, and more than 3,000 Sisters and Novices, still follow the example of her work in teaching and nursing.

When she died, the liberated slaves in Mana held a week of public mourning and a statue was erected to her in their Church square. The inscription reads:

"Anne-Marie Javouhey: 1779 - 1851.
She was the Foundress and the Mother of Mana."

The long and complex road to Anne-Marie's Beatification began in 1908, and passed through many levels of discussion and formalities. Finally, on the 15th October, 1950, almost one hundred years after her death, Pope Pius XII pronounced Anne-Marie Javouhey Blessed.

Much has been written about Blessed Anne-Marie Javouhey, and her own letters are quoted and reproduced over and over for the communities who still follow her example and teachings today.

However, Emily Bronte, writing in Anne-Marie's own era, penned these words, which are titled quite simply *"Last Lines"* -

> *"No coward soul is mine,*
> *No trembler in the world's storm-troubled sphere;*
> *I see Heaven's glories shine,*
> *And faith shines equal, arming me from fear..."*

Perhaps this is as fitting a memorial as any to this truly extraordinary woman.

The arrival of the Cluny Congregation in Ireland

"We have been asked to go to Ireland, to teach the poor and the well-to-do. I have been assured that we could do much good there. If such be the will of God, I agree to this foundation with all my heart."

Blessed Anne-Marie wrote the above in 1850. However, it was to be ten years before the congregation was to set foot on Irish soil. At the invitation of Dr. Cullen, Archbishop of Dublin, following a recommendation and perhaps a little persuasion from Rev. Fr. J. Leman CSSP, three French nuns, of whom Sister Callixte Pichet was leader, arrived in Ireland on the 12th of December 1860.

Sr. Callixte Pichet
Rev. Mother 1860 - 1888

Sister Callixte was born in Cluny in 1823 and was professed at a young age. She began her missionary vocation at the age of eighteen, when she was sent to the island of Martinique. On her return to Europe in 1852, she spent a number of years gaining experience in well- known educational establishments throughout France, after which she spent a period in Rome. She returned to her missionary activities abroad in the late 1850's, when she was posted to Reunion in the Indian Ocean. It was from this post in 1860 that Mother Callixte was sent to Dublin via Paris, where she was to collect two companions.

The three sisters took up residence in a rather dilapidated old Carmelite Monastery, located near the church in Blanchardstown. This beautifully restored stone building still survives today. It is at present occupied by a number of small businesses and a Thai Restaurant. Until recently, it was the premises of Brennan's Kitchens. The building was originally St. Brigid's Seminary. In those days a seminary was an educational establishment which usually produced a number of vocations for the priesthood or religious life. In 1828 the building was entrusted by the Most Rev. Doctor Murray, Archbishop of Dublin to four Carmelite Sisters, who founded 'the Convent of the Incarnation' there. The four sisters, Mother Mary Francis de Sales, Sister Agnes Rafter, Sister Mary Paul Doyle and novice Teresa Joseph Mc Donald were transferred from Firhouse to Blanchardstown.

Almost four years later, the convent experienced difficulties and was closed on the 1st of March 1832. However, the Carmelites maintained their connection with the school until 1858. After the departure of the sisters, it seems that the building was unoccupied for a number of years. In 1859 Father Ignatius Schwindenhammer of the Holy Ghost Fathers in France sent a Father Leman, two other priests and two brothers to set up another Seminary in Blanchardstown. This was with the view to finding vocations for the missions. This proved very successful and within a year, the demand for applications was so great, that there was a need to move to a larger premises. The Holy Ghost Fathers purchased a former Protestant Boarding School in Blackrock, on the south side of the city. The premises was later extended to include a school and was renamed the French College of the Immaculate Heart of Mary, now better known as Blackrock College. On the 12th of December 1860, the sisters of Saint Joseph of Cluny set up a convent in the former Seminary in Blanchardstown. Sister Callixte described their furniture as consisting of *"four beds,one deal table and some chairs"* while in their chapel they had *"an old wooden altar"* without any tabernacle or altar stone. The sisters resided there until they moved to Mount Sackville in 1864.

Blanchardstown, c1900 Original house where sisters settled in 1860
Illustration by Orla Walsh, third year student

The former Carmelite Convent in Blanchardstown, now a Thai Restaurant and home to a number of small businesses, where Mother Callixte and her companions settled on the 12th December 1860.

On the night of her arrival she wrote this letter to her superior in France, describing their journey via London and her arrival at Blanchardstown:

*   *   *   *

Blanchardstown, Co. Dublin
Thursday night, Dec. 12th 1860

My very dear Mother,

In spite of the fact that we are very tired, I don't want to go to bed without giving you news of our voyage, and of our arrival here this a.m. at 8 o'clock, as we expected, although we were delayed and had to stay in Dieppe for more than eight hours to wait for the wind and sea to calm a little; We had to go to the hotel at midnight through storms and downpours. The next morning at 9 o'clock, the Captain who had promised to let us know if the wind was calming, sent for us, and we embarked immediately although the weather wasn't much better. We wanted to try and stay on deck because on these wretched little steamers, the second class passengers had no privacy inside, much less a bed to sleep on. However, although they were good enough to cover us from head to toe in big blankets we couldn't remain on deck more than a quarter of an hour. The sea was furious and the waves thrown in on the deck inundated us continually. It wasn't possible to stay there. As for me I was so terribly sea-sick, there was no means of holding out, and when I saw my two companions almost as sick as I was with this wretched malady, I decided immediately to ask for places in the first-class lounge, offering to pay extra, which was willingly granted to us for five francs each. We continued to be sick; the sea was too rough for to be otherwise, but at least we were sheltered from the rain and the wind and the strong waves. Apart from that, our voyage couldn't have been better.

Everyone in London and everywhere else, showed us great respect; they looked at us but only from a distance, and even with more respect than curiosity. Everywhere we were given carriages for ourselves alone, and when they wanted to put even a lady in our carriage, they asked our permission as if all the places were ours. From London to Dublin the fare seemed costly to us - 220 francs for the three of us. And so we arrived here this morning. The Irish sea was not near as rough as the Channel, and at 8 o'clock when leaving the boat we met the good Father Holley who was waiting for us, and so we arrived at our destination. Father Holley conducted us to the college (Blackrock) where we had something to eat. Father Leman was also very good to us. Father Holley came with us to show us our house (Blanchardstown) as well as the provisions that he had arranged to be taken there for us.

When we arrived a considerable crowd of little boys followed our carriage, but they looked more happy than curious. We wanted to make a visit to the church, even before entering the house, but the parish priest who had been notified of our arrival, came to meet us and took us to the Parochial House so as to avoid the crowd. On every side women and children were running about the village.

The parish priest and Father Holley accompanied us to our Convent, and immediately offered to say Mass for us the following morning. Unfortunately the Chapel is bereft of furniture, with the exception of a wooden altar, no statues nor tabernacle, no altar stone, nothing. Father Holley will buy us a cheap tabernacle here, and he hopes that you will provide us with the other essentials.

Adieu, my good Mother. It is getting late and I am very tired. My very best wishes to all. I hardly know what I am writing, but you will be good enough to excuse the scribble because of our fatigue. Adieu. Your three Irish daughters embrace you with all their hearts.

Yours affectionately,
Sister Callixte.

*   *   *   *

The Ireland of the 1860s experienced post famine problems, such as poverty, disease, emigration and above all disillusionment. There were five million people living on the island, four million of whom were directly or indirectly linked to farming. All the land belonged to ten thousand landlords, most of whom were Protestant. The majority of the population were tenants, who lived in severe poverty and constant fear of eviction. Young people were more prone to put their trust in secret societies which plotted armed rebellion, than in constitutional politics. Until 1869 the Church of Ireland was the established church and enjoyed many privileges, such as the receipt of tithes i.e. taxes the tenant farmers had to pay. It owned church property, schools and hospitals. Trinity College, the only university in Ireland until the 1840s was mainly an Anglican institution where clergymen were trained. University education was the prerogative of the non- Catholic middle-class. Many children finished school at the age of ten or eleven to work on the farm or to get a job in industries such as milling, brewing, baking or distilling. Most secondary schools were for boys. Very few girls were educated, as the general attitude was that a woman's place was in the home. Those who were educated came from a middle class background. Upon leaving school many worked in secretarial positions or devoted their lives to God, by joining a religious order. It was against this background that Mother Pichet took up residence in Blanchardstown. Although extreme poverty reigned in Blanchardstown at the time and although the sisters spoke no English, twenty three Irish girls joined their community within the first year.

The Community continued to expand rapidly, with requests for admissions arriving daily. The premises in Blanchardstown however was unsuitable for a larger congregation. With the view to opening a girls' secondary school, Mother Callixte looked for a more suitable residence. Having first considered a property at Monkstown, they soon discovered that the more attractive demesne of Mount Sackville had come up for sale.

After much persuasive letter writing to higher superiors to extract both the permission and money to buy it, Mount Sackville became the property of the sisters of Joseph of Cluny in January 1864, purchased for a sum of 70,000 francs, €10,000.

Mount Sackville, 1864

Convent Chapel in Mount Sackville, 1877

In January 1864, Mother Callixte wrote the following to her Superior General in France:

> *"We must give up the idea of this property in Monkstown'....I have found better than that, that is to say a property, three times bigger with a beautiful house where I am sure to be able to lodge.... at least thirty boarders....it is called 'Uplands' but if you wish we will call it St. Joseph's Lands....There is a fine garden, lovely walks planted with more than 100 oak trees and many other things that will please the children and the parents. All are unanimous in promising us great success in our <u>new boarding School</u>."*

In a further letter to her Mother General dated 20th February 1864, sister Callixte explains how:

> *"St. Joseph's Lands cannot be the name of the house for many reasons which have been weighed by our friends and by people who are better judges of the matter than I! We shall speak of it and write Mount Sackville because this is the name by which all or nearly all the Catholic families know this beautiful estate"*

Some Local History

Mrs Carroll, a lady from the Strawberry beds, wrote the following in 1885:

Mount Sackville Convent is at the head, Where young ladies, they are bred,
And taught by nuns of every form, The duties women's life adorn.
Beside it, Mr. Guinness built a tower. It has a clock strike every hour.
It can be heard from far and near; And gives the working people cheer:
It lets them know the time to quit; They may go home and eat their bit;
Near to that is the seat of knowledge, At Castleknock's St. Vincent's College........

A Candle in the window
By J Lacey

The Strawberry Beds

The road from Knockmaroon along the banks of the Liffey to Lucan was noted for strawberry cultivation on the south facing slopes, hence the name. This area was a popular tourist resort when Mount Sackville was established in the nineteenth century. The population of Dublin travelled every Sunday afternoon, by pony and trap or by jaunting car, to sample the luscious strawberries (which could be bought wrapped in a cabbage leaf), after which they took a stroll by Anna Livia or washed down the strawberries in the local hostelries, the Anglers' Rest, The Strawberry Hall and the Wren's Nest.

The Phoenix Park, which adjoins the grounds of Mount Sackville in the early 1900's.

The Strawberry Beds by the River Liffey in the 19th century

Farmleigh

The estate of Farmleigh adjoins the grounds of Mount Sackville. It is noted for its clock tower, which is visible for miles around. This estate of seventy eight acres, is located on both sides of the River Liffey. The house was purchased from the Guinness family by the Irish Government in 1999.

Originally a small Georgian house built in the late 18th Century, Farmleigh was purchased by Edward Cecil Guinness (1847-1927) on his marriage to his cousin, Adelaide Guinness in 1873. Edward was a great grandson of Arthur Guinness, founder of the Guinness Brewery, Edward Cecil became the first Earl of Iveagh in 1919. Down through the years the Guinness Family proved to be good neighbours and friends of Mount Sackville. In fact the late Sr. Eugene Mc Cabe used to walk up through the fields to teach music to the children of the Late Lord Iveagh. The house has been carefully refurbished by the Office of Public Works as the premier accommodation for visiting dignitaries and for important government meetings, such as those during Ireland's Presidency of the EU.

Farmleigh in 1873

Chapelizod

There is much controversy about the origin of the name Chapelizod. It is said that the town/village was named after a beautiful Irish Princess called Isolde. However, the late President Douglas Hyde suggested the name came from Seipéal Easóige (Stoats Chapel) while an intellectual John O'Donovan claims in favour of Seipéal Iseal. Whatever the origin of its name, Chapelizod has a long and interesting history.

Sir Henry Power, later known as Lord Valentia, an Elizabethan adventurer, had his house built in this village, where the present day industrial estate is situated. William III is said to have lived in the same house during the Battle of the Boyne. In the 1670's a Colonel Lawrence encouraged the Duke of Ormonde to set up a new industry in the town for the manufacturing of linen and woollen goods. The Lovett family later ran this business - Christopher Lovett served a period as Lord Mayor of Dublin while his wife was the sister-in-law of John Knox, the well-known religious reformer during the Reformation. The Linen mill was later operated by a Mr Crosthwaite who employed several hundred people in the locality.

William Dargan opened a mill for spinning linen in Chapelizod in the 1850s. However, the mill was sold to a Distillery Company in 1878. A huge fire destroyed it in 1901, however, it resumed production for a short while after that but never regained its former success. Today it is the site of an apartment development.

Chapelizod also has links to James Joyce. In fact the Mullingar House is the setting for James Joyce's masterpiece *'Finnegans Wake'*, Mount Sackville is referred to in the novel, in that the daughters of Mr Earwicker, the publican, attended school there.

Castleknock College

Castleknock College was purchased in 1834 by Rev. John McCann, on behalf of the Vincentian community.

A castle was built there during Norman times by Hugh Tyrrell. The site was carefully chosen, located at the highest point between the Liffey and the

Tolka. It commanded the route into Dublin from the west. In 1666 the castle and land became the property of a distinguished Norman family, the Warrens of Corduff and was eventually bought by Rev. William Gwynn, who set up a seminary here for young Protestant gentlemen. Castleknock College has among its past pupils, many well known clergy, sportsmen and academics. Queen Victoria visited the College during her visit to Ireland in 1900.

Chapelizod, c1900

View of the ruins of Castleknock Castle, 1791
Picture courtesy of Jim Lacey

The history of the House and Origin of the name Mount Sackville

From its probable establishment in the middle of the eighteenth century, it is likely that Mount Sackville was named after Lord George Sackville, later known as Lord Germain. George Sackville was born on the 26th of January 1716 and was the third son of Lionel Cranfield Sackville, the first Duke of Dorset and twice Lord Lieutenant of Ireland. There were two well known Dublin streets named after this man, Sackville Street (now O'Connell Street) and Dorset Street.

George had two careers. His military career had some distinction, but ended with a court martial. His political career ended with the North ministry after the loss of the American colonies. George is said to have attended Trinity College and joined the British Army in 1737. He fought in Fontenoy in 1745 and later in the battle of Minden in 1759, where he refused to obey orders and as such was sent back to England, where he was court martialled. The court ruled that he was *"unfit to serve his Majesty in any capacity what-so-ever"*.

On his return to Ireland he acted as his father's Chief Secretary during his second Vice-Royalty and he was appointed ranger in the Phoenix Park in 1761. It is during this time that he may have lived in Mount Sackville. He represented Portarlington in the House of Commons and was appointed Colonial Secretary.

In 1769 Lady Elizabeth Germain, an elderly and very rich lady, died without natural heirs and left her estate to him, on condition that he take the name Germain. So from 1770, he was known as George, Lord Germain.

On his retirement in 1782 he was given the title Viscount Sackville and he died in Kent on the 26th August 1785. Sackville's son succeeded to the Dukeship of Dorset on the death of John, Duke of Dorset, his first cousin, who was killed in 1815, while hunting at Killiney Hill, Dublin.

Sackville is reputed to have been a man of great intelligence and one of the best orators of his time in the House of Commons. According to many historians, e.g. Thackeray, he is said to have been proud and arrogant. However, in his private life he appears to have been good and kind.

The house, which is now Mount Sackville was occupied by a Thomas Kemnis in 1801, whose family were well distinguished in the legal profession in Ireland at that time. The proprietor and occupant of the house prior to 1843 was a Mr. John Hawkins, who remained the main proprietor for many years, after he let the house. In fact, it is likely that he was the proprietor when the sisters purchased the property in 1864.

From 1843-1860 Mount Sackville was occupied by a William Walmesley. It seems the house was rented by him from Hawkins. From 1860-1864 it was occupied by Lt. Colonel Henry Holden of the regiment of the 13th Dragoons. The property of Mount Sackville adjoined the beautiful estate of Lord Iveagh.

Lord Cranfield Sackville, First Duke of Dorset and father of George Sackville

The early years and the Establishment of the Boarding School

Mother Callixte Pichet and her companions moved into Mount Sackville on the 25th February 1864. She was a remarkable woman, with unbounded organisational skills, and straight away set about reshaping and extending Mount Sackville.

Father Ebenrecht of Blackrock College was her architect. She herself was clerk of works. Soon, under her energetic supervision, cloisters, dormitories and an infirmary sprang up. A big shed was converted into a recreational hall for boarders. A large and beautiful chapel was erected in 1877.

From the beginning of its foundations. Sr. Callixte spoke of the need to have teachers of English and French and especially German. She also suggested in her earlier letters to the Mother House, the need to have a good musician and a good teacher for handwork, especially 'fancy needlework', and if possible an Art Teacher.

It appears that her wishes were fulfilled, as volume II of the 1889 edition of the bulletin issued by the congregation, records the visit to the school of the Archbishop of Dublin, Msg. Walsh. The students performed piano pieces and songs and used French dialogue to welcome His Grace. They presented him with a framed piece of embroidery, consisting of a picture of His Grace and his coat of arms. The Archbishop complimented the girls on their very good French accents.

Sister Callixte, was Mother Superior in Mount Sackville until 1888 when she was recalled to the mother house in Paris. She was succeeded by Mother Gabriel Horner, an Alsatian lady, recorded in the 1901 census as German (from the time of the Franco-Prussian war in 1870 Alsace had been annexed by Germany, not to be returned to France until 1919). She was a wise superior and a successful teacher of German, the language of her childhood. Mount Sackville National School was established in 1890. By 1893 it seems Mount Sackville had 47 boarders and 87 day pupils and by 1896, the national school had 122 pupils and 16 postulants. The number of boarders had also increased. The bulletin of that year records, that the school produced very good exam results and that the inspector was very pleased.

The 1899 Bulletin noted the excellent exam results and how a subvention given from the Mother House in France had amounted to 4,500 francs that year. Exams in those days were usually set by the school and were sometimes geared towards gaining entrance to the Civil Service or universities abroad.

Mary Glennon & Elizabeth Glennon were students in the 1880's

Mary Glennon and Elizabeth Glennon

The above photograph shows two girls at school in Mount Sackville, in their uniforms, back in the 1880s. They were sisters, Mary Glennon on the left and Elizabeth Glennon from Hardwood House, Kinnegad, Co Westmeath.

Elizabeth later married a Mr. Paddy Connolly and had several children.

Mary married a Mr. Tom O'Connor and had ten children - two of whom became priests and two became nuns.

The two Mount Sackville girls had two famous brothers. One named John, the eldest of the family became Cardinal John Glennon of St. Louis in the USA. He had become Archbishop of St. Louis in 1903, thereby becoming the youngest Archbishop ever in the history of the American Catholic Church. He organised the building of a magnificent Cathedral in St. Louis, which is in the Byzantine style. He was made a Cardinal in 1946, but died shortly afterwards in Dublin aged eighty four.

The girls' other famous brother was William Glennon, a surgeon who also lived in St. Louis. He completed over 50,000 operations during his life. People of St. Louis used to say of the brothers *"John will look after your soul and William your health"*.

One hundred years later, another two Glennon sisters, Carina and Mairead, great grand-nieces of Mary and Elizabeth, were pupils in Mount Sackville and in the 1990's another two sisters, Katherine and Emily O'Callaghan, daughters of Pauline O'Callaghan, a teacher in Mount Sackville, also grand-nieces of Mary and Elizabeth, were pupils in Mount Sackville.

According to the 1901 census, (see appendix) Mount Sackville had 75 students boarding and employed eighteen teachers, some of whom originated in France and Germany. It also records twelve manual labourers living here at the time, two of whom were from France, two from Germany, one from England and the remainder from Ireland.

Among the pupils of 1901, one was as young as four years old, named Mary Roche, a native of Dublin City. The two oldest students were Hannah O'Brien from Co.Cork who was aged twenty nine and Mary Somers from Co. Limerick who was aged twenty eight. In fact Hannah O'Brien was older than the youngest teacher who was twenty four years old, Winifred O'Connell, a native of Co. Louth.

By 1901 exams seem to have become more difficult. However, students in Mount Sackville won several prizes. Two received 500 francs and others between 25 and 100. 11,900 francs were paid to the school by the Education Department in 1901. A boarding school had inspectors like all the government schools and in October 1901 two inspectors visited the school to observe the teachers' performance. The inspectors were extremely pleased with both teacher performance and the discipline in the school. It was around this time that Irish was introduced as a subject. Irish as a native language had declined rapidly after the Famine and had almost disappeared in some parts of the country. The foundation of the Gaelic League in 1893 by Douglas Hyde and Eoin MacNeill helped to revive the language and prevent its decline. On its introduction, the students in Mount Sackville are recorded as having picked it up quickly and the school won prizes for Irish.

A fascinating insight into the social mores of the time is provided by the not untypical story of Selina Leader. Her father, Leonard Henry Leader was the son of Thomas Leader, and was born in Cork. His religion was Roman Catholic. He was called to the Irish Bar in 1842. His only child Selina, was six years old when he died. Her mother was also dead and her father had left her all his money. A family friend, Richard (Dick) Kavanagh, possibly her god-father, gave her a home in his Dublin house and subsequently sent her as a boarder to Mount Sackville. He reputedly used to visit her at the school in a coach, but according to family legend, she never left the school, even for holidays, for eleven years. In 1876, when she was seventeen years old, a man called Thomas Kavanagh (no relation of Richard) came to Mount Sackville School with a friend to visit that friend's sister. He met Selina and put his eye on her. He worked in the legal Department of the Dublin Gas Company and is described on the Marriage Certificate as a Law Clerk. They got married in Haddington Road Church on 13/09/1876. They had nine children, all of whom survived into adulthood.

Apparently it was quite common for young ladies to be married from the school, as happened to her.

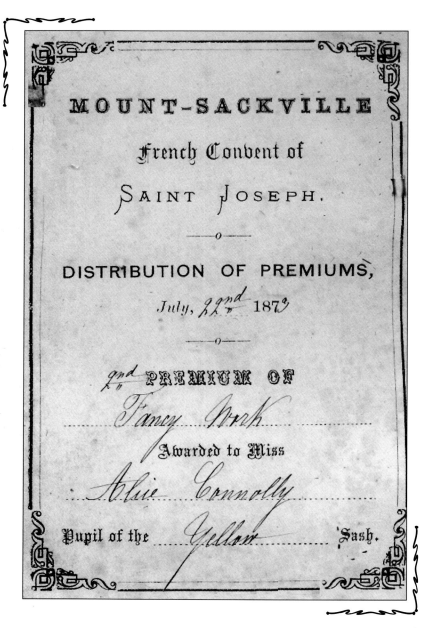

MOUNT-SACKVILLE

French Convent of

SAINT JOSEPH.

— o —

DISTRIBUTION OF PREMIUMS,

July, 22nd 1873

— o —

2nd **PREMIUM OF**

Fancy Work

Awarded to Miss

Alice Connolly

Pupil of the *Yellow* Sash.

Prize Certificate, 1873

Pupils in 1909

The Orchestra, c1900

The Junior School

In 1905 a red-brick building was erected and equipped, in which fifty young boys aged from four to twelve years were boarded and educated. Known then as *'The Boys School'* it soon catered for small girls too, who were taught in separate classes. However, when the number of girls dwindled it was decided that they would attend the national school (Scoil Mhuire) and continue to board in Mount Sackville. In the mid 1950's there was a polio scare and it was feared that the girls would be more at risk of contracting the malady through contact with day pupils in the national school. So it was decided that the girls who were boarding would join the classes in *'the boys' school'*. As time passed, the number of boys dwindled and the vacant places were quickly filled by girls, some of them boarders and others day pupils. Eventually the name of the school changed to *'The Junior School'*, which stayed in operation until it closed its doors for the last time in 1996. The late William Walsh was a past pupil of the boys' school. He attended Mount Sackville when Ireland was in the grip of the War of Independence and the Civil War. He remembers the Black and Tans taking up their position on the convent walls. By kind permission of Mrs. Walsh and the Blarney Magazine, the sisters were allowed to reproduce this article written by him in remembrance of his days in Mount Sackville:

*   *   *   *

Boyhood in a Dublin Convent
By William Walsh

The Convent was situated at the most wooded, secluded side of the Phoenix Park, and according to the notice erected on wooden supports inside the surrounding wall was for *"Young Ladies and Little Boys."* I went there as a little boy at the age of five, joining my two brothers and my sister, all older than I, who were already pupils.

I can remember well the drive to the Convent with my mother in the old, horse-drawn cab through the Phoenix Park, already filled with the sadness of a September afternoon. Our trunks were piled on the top of the cab, and this evidence of a long separation from our home in Kildare was strong enough to fill us all, including my mother, who was as simple as ourselves, with the choking loneliness which I was ever afterwards to associate with going away to school. But I had begged to be allowed to go and I could only accept my loneliness as part of the price to be paid for the distinction of being at school.

The boys' part of the school was, of course, separate, and really only constituted of a few large rooms, but inside those walls was an organisation strong enough to imprint on one's mind forever, correct ideas of moral and physical wellbeing.

I do not quite remember the routine of our days, but I know that life was intensely serious for us. One nun took charge of our health and the shaping of our moral instincts, and I do not think in my whole life I ever came across a person of greater character. We were awakened in the morning by the clapping of her hands, and she was very expert in making the soft bed of her palms meet in a resounding smack.

We, of course, attended Mass in the mornings, and to do so had to pass into the girls' school through long passages, down corridors hushed through the years by the silence of hundreds of humbled nuns. Even the oak floors, waxed and polished though they were, seemed softened by the padding of thousands of felted footsteps. We filed to the place in the chapel allotted to us and, though we seemed countless then, there were only about twenty of us. Of the girls in their white lace veils, without which formal covering it would have been a great sin to go into Chapel, we took little notice, except those of us who had sisters. However, I remember the romantic figure of one of the oldest girls in the school whose sister was said to be engaged to Michael Collins, then at the height of his fame as a leader in the Irish Revolutionary Movement.

In the summer we played cricket in the Phoenix Park. When I first went to the convent, we were not allowed a real cricket ball, because it was thought to be dangerous, but played with a leather ball. Later on, a young nun - more daring - was in charge of games, and she succeeded in procuring a real cricket ball, but the wise Reverend Mother ordained that the ball should lie on the Chapel altar for a week so that the blessings of Masses and other prayers would fall on it and take the dangers out of it. That faith which invoked God's aid for personal and very trifling material ends was in me too, for I prayed very vigorously that I should be enabled to find a goldfinch's nest, which I did not do, at least until so much later that I would be justified in doubting if it was the result of my prayers.

Every year we had an annual Retreat. It was given in September shortly after reopening, and the echoing of a preacher's voice still brings back memories of those thin days of shortening evenings, when the Convent grounds became bedded with red beech and yellow chestnut leaves, and the only consolation was playing "Champions" with the great mahogany-coloured chestnuts. At the Retreat, the underlying note of the lectures was the dangers of the world outside. No doubt, compared to the secluded life inside the Convent walls, there were many temptations outside, but I must say I have never found the passage-ways of life lined with such tempting sins as were hinted at in those lectures.

One of the things we little boys were constantly urged to do by the nuns at that time was to pray for Ireland. All we knew was that outside there was political storm, shooting and destruction, and we saw many signs in the Phoenix Park of British military activity. The nuns did not burden us with the merits of the issue, but contented themselves with urging us to pray, as I think they themselves were content to pray, for Ireland, generally. Though there was much shooting and ambushing not far distant, no one molested us, and the nearest we ever came to the conflict was one morning after the attack on the Lord Lieutenant's entourage at Ashtown, two Black and Tans* who had taken up their position on the convent walls spoke down to us, and asked us where were the big girls. The nuns were non-political, though, I remember when some clergymen visited us we were primed to ask for Archbishop Mannix, who was unknown to us, but who I know now, had raised his voice for Ireland. On the other hand, when a parent, a Major in the British Army, who had served with distinction in 1914-1918, called to see his son, he was respectfully entertained, and we were brought out to run up and down for his approval. He was a fine figure of a man, as he paced the playground with the nun in charge, in his uniform decorated with bar and badge.

It is hard to think that one could suffer much unhappiness in those sheltered surroundings, but wherever there are boys bigger than others there will be oppression, though I was considerably protected by having two brothers among the bigger boys. But of happiness there was plenty. Certainly, I cannot recall ever having tasted happiness to satiety like on those summer evenings which, in recollection, seemed warmer and longer than any that have come since, when we came back from truancy, bird-nesting at the lake - a bush-encircled pond, and on the mountain, a hill on the convent's farm, where a Calvary was erected. We came in, panting, to fill our places in the refectory before Grace, ready to make the most of the

* The Black and Tans (British Government Forces) fought the I.R.A. during the War of Independance, 1920

44

home-made brown bread which was carried in fresh from the oven in a large wicker basket.

Great was the apprehension in the refectory one Saturday evening when the curly-headed boy we called Rebel came in late to tea. Word had come through earlier that he had been apprehended in the adjoining estate interfering with a pheasant's nest in search of an egg for his collection. Never in war or in peace did a raid seem more daring, or the sought-for prize more rare and unattainable. We all admired Rebel's intrepid effort, and though I was far below his notice, the memory of his gallant figure with the evening sun glinting on his fair curls and summer freckled face, as he stood in conference in the playground with two of his associates, is with me still. His transgression appeared enormous and unforgivable, and more so, when the next evening the Reverend Mother addressed us in the Refectory, and spoke of the disgrace he had brought on us all by his act, offensive to a gentleman to whose kindness and goodwill we owed so much enjoyment. Apparently, we were very much under this gentleman's shadow, as we understood he could, if he wished, crush the whole convent, nuns, grounds and all, in his wealthy grasp.

I cannot say I remember Rebel receiving any punishment beyond stigmatisation-which in the case of his friends amounted to glorification - for it was well known that his bold, sunny face was beloved by the brave nun who fed and kept us clean, and as he was leaving school that term any-way, perhaps indecision extended for the few weeks until break-up, when he marched away to the wicked life which we were told surely awaited him.

Rebel's parents always visited the convent in their motor car, driven by a chauffeur, and as only few and wealthy people had cars in those days, we clustered round the car and chauffeur while Rebel and his parents walked around the grounds. The registration of that car was IK-1988 and when asked what this meant, the chauffeur assured us that it meant *"I killed 1988 chickens,"* and that he had put the lettering and numbers up to let this be known!

My brothers and I were in no way wild, but very sensible, and the eldest looked after the rest with paternal solicitude. I know that in the winter he had a porter bottle which he somehow managed to fill with warm water, and having warmed his toes would pass it on to my next eldest brother, who in turn would pass the bottle on to me. My eldest brother, it was well-known, was to take over our farm in Kildare as soon as at all possible, and the nun in charge frequently sent him out to the farmyard to do odd jobs. He was always sent out late on summer evenings to put in the ducks, as *"how else,"* used Sister to say, *"would he be able to look after things at home, if he did not take an interest.*"

Perhaps our days in the convent cannot seriously be described as 'at school,' but it was not so to us, or those in charge of us. Every tiny aspect of our routine was taken as seriously as if it were part of preparation for a University degree, and certainly, no one at home could equal the kind, but firm supervision of our wellbeing and instruction.

During the influenza epidemic in 1920, we were as cut off from the outside world as if we had been on a desert island. Even the letters we received from home were not given us, but were read to us, after they had been sprinkled with disinfectant, lest they should carry contagion.

It must certainly have influenced our lives that we had the beautiful tree-shaded park to play in, though we were under threat that this also would be lost to us by any impropriety. Once, some boy broke the branch of a tree, and again enormous guilt fell on the school. We were told that we had the liberty of the park only through the generosity of the park keeper, and surely, if we broke another branch his patience would give out.

Our portion of the grounds held charms and opportunities for adventure too, though the nuns tried to sanctify them by a statue in the very centre. I am afraid we played around this statue with very little sense of its spiritual significance. It was of St. Rock, a saint with whom I must confess I have long ceased to be acquainted. We also had a tall cypress tree with branches spreading down like the prisms of a chandelier, its peak tapering finely to the sky and it afforded an exalted stage to the bravest singing blackbird I have ever known. An outspread palm tree at the end of the playground near the convent wall was a hiding place for those who had purposes to conceal. Fights to end differences took place behind the palm tree. They were rare and forbidden, and I know that my brother was sentenced to be kept back two days after break-up for being an observer, duly identified, of such a fight.

But all was not noise in those grounds, and they were serene and beautiful on many evenings. I remember such an evening in June when we little boys headed to a Corpus Christi procession. Dressed in white, we scattered flower petals in front of the host as the procession made its way along the sheltered walks to the Calvary on the Mountain, and back. We were followed by the white-veiled girls singing the Latin hymns, their pure voices filling the air, already rich with incense, in honour of the sacred feast we commemorated.

Though many things have changed since I was a little boy, I imagine the scenes inside the convent are much the same. I hope so anyway, and every June it seems to me still that the procession goes on, unending, past strewn flowers, in an atmosphere of incense and singing children, and along the walks and paths given up to sanctity and peace.

*   *   *   *

In 1910, a hall was built for childrens' concerts and theatre. Music seemed to have been well-established in Mount Sackville. At the time, the number of pupils in special choir was as high as fifty. Individuals excelled themselves in music and singing. The Orchestra was well equipped and had at its disposal fifteen violins, three violoncello, two violas, a drum, a triangle, a flute and a piano.

In the early twentieth century, the number of girls entering religious life was extremely high. This fact was very much reflected in Mount Sackville. In 1910, ten pupils entered religious life, eight of them becoming Sisters of Saint Joseph of Cluny.

The 1911 census records forty four Sisters residing in the convent. While the majority were Irish in origin, some came from Portugal, Germany and France. The Secondary School had sixty-nine pupils while twelve boys resided in the Boys' School.

During World War I, 1914-1918, Mount Sackville had one hundred and twenty boarders. Poverty and hardship were widespread on both a national and global level. In keeping with the school's motto, *"Faith, Hope and Charity"*, the students were quick to respond. Proceeds from the annual concerts went towards helping the poverty-stricken, including the Belgian refugees. While the 1916 Rising disrupted students somewhat, the exam results at the end of that year proved satisfactory.

With the establishment of the Free State in 1921, and the introduction of the Intermediate Education Act of 1923 by the Cumann na nGaedhael Government, the Leaving Certificate and Intermediate Certificate (later replaced by the Junior Cert) became a necessary part of school life. Teaching proved more demanding and the teachers in Mount Sackville, like elsewhere in the country, had to complete courses in Dublin during the school holidays.

Religious Education exams were also set up by diocesan priests, and by 1938, the congregation bulletin records the importance of both written and oral exams in Catechism, Church History, Gospel Studies and Catholic Action. The Legion of Mary was inaugurated in the school in 1936 and proved to be a huge success. The bulletin also records the outstanding achievements of the pupils in public exams. Forty-five students passed the Matriculation. This was an exam set by the National University of Ireland and Trinity College. It was taken after the Leaving Certificate to gain entrance to university. Many were successful in both Leaving and Intermediate exams.

Mount Sackville, 1924

Mount Sackville in the 1920's & 30's

The main staircase in Mount Sackville as it looked in the 1930's

Sister Cecilia Kenny from Ferbane, Offaly and Sister William Pillion from Clonmacnois were both boarders in Mount Sackville from the mid 30's to 1940. On completion of their Secondary Education in Mount Sackville they, like so many before them and so many later, were destined to become Sisters of St. Joseph of Cluny and to spend approximately sixty years - one in the Seychelles and the other in India.

As boarders, they have memories of the vibrant practice of their Faith which included daily Mass, May devotions, recitation of the Rosary and occasionally, some senior girls participated in the Prayer of the Church with the Sisters. They note the many boarders and the few day pupils in the school in the 1930's.

The Sisters take the students to Laytown, Co. Meath.
during the summer holidays, 1939

In passing we mention that the 30's was the beginning of an era when Irish girls were about to take their place in the new 'Free State'. Sr. Cecilia mentions the preparation done with those girls who wanted to enter the Civil Service. A West Indian Sister taught them music and their memory of Science is the skeleton that was the *piéce de résistance* of the Science Room. Saturdays were devoted to Ballroom Dancing, Drill, visits to the City and the Phoenix Park. Sr. Cecilia recalls an Air Show in the Park, made memorable because some of the girls smoked and compounded the transgression by being caught! She also recalls the visit of the first woman pilot who crossed the Atlantic and signed autographs for the students.

A Pageant staged by the pupils in 1928

Back Row: Bridie Kelly, Lettie Curley, Lilian Roberts (Finlay), Connie Condron, [Unidentified], Jessie Cussens,

Margaret Lawless

Front Row: Peggie Bowles, Louise Sweeney and Eileen Sweeney

Pupils in 1930
Back Row: Muriel Cussens, Selina Grimes, Monica Curley
Front Row: Ada Moses (now Sr. Germaine), Louise Sweeney, Peggie Bowles
and Breda O'Donnell

Mount Sackville Boys in 1929
Back Row, 4th from the left: Derry Sweeney (now a Vincentian Priest)

Another exciting event of those days was a visit by Maureen O'Hara to one of the Phoenix Park Lodges. They caught a glimpse of her on horseback in the Park. Sports, then as now, were very much part of the education programme. All played hockey and tennis in the grounds. Cricket was played in the Phoenix Park!

One other memory is that of a daily walk in the Park. It was common practice to invite Sisters home on leave from the 'mission countries' to address the students regarding their work overseas. It was accepted that students who for one reason or another could not go home joined the Sisters on their holidays at the sea side, or occasionally accompanied the Sisters home on holidays to their family.

Colm O'Regan, a past pupil of The Boys' School on the day he received his First Holy Communion, 1939

Mount Sackville in the 1940's

In helping me to establish a picture of Mount Sackville in the 1940's and 1950's, I would like to thank Sister Colm Keane who kindly allowed me to interview her.

Sister Colm Keane, a native of Co Galway, joined the teaching staff of Mount Sackville in 1943. She spent forty one years teaching in Scoil Mhuire National School. During this time she also taught Maths and her first love, Music, in the secondary school. A violinist, she was responsible for reviving the orchestra. She availed of the many musical instruments at her disposal, including a cello, a double bass, violins and violas. Through her dedication and commitment, her endeavours were soon rewarded by the establishment of a very successful school orchestra of thirty students, who were successful in exams.

'The Arcadians' performed on 12th November 1946 in Mount Sackville.
Philomena Scully (desceased), Freda O'Connor (deceased), Aine Leary (now Twomey), Bridie O'Kelly (now O'Connor), Madeleine McLoughlin (now Kelly)

In 1943 there were sixty boarders in the secondary school and about eighty in the primary school. A large percentage of the girls went on to enter the religious life, many in Ferbane. There were only a few day pupils. She recalls the first student to travel to school by motor car. She was a member of the Massey Family, from Inchicore, proprietors of a well established printing company at the time.

The teaching staff were all Sisters. Among them was Sister Ursula Garvey, who was Mistress of Studies and a History teacher. Sister Berchmans Ryan taught Music, English and French. Sister Clothilde Gallagher taught Latin, Sister Henry McArdle taught Geography, Sister Aloysius O'Reilly taught Domestic Science, and gave politeness lessons. The Mother Superior and Provincial at the time was Mother Paul Molloy. She was an energetic and remarkable woman, who worked closely with the other Sisters. She also taught Maths. The first lay teachers arrived in the 1950's.

Boarders in those days returned home only during holiday time, Christmas, Easter and Summer. Gradually by the 60's they were allowed home once a month.

Sister Colm remembers how it was sometimes difficult to occupy the boarders at weekends. Every Saturday they would be taught etiquette, drawing and elocution and were active in the Legion of Mary.

Every day began with Mass. The girls would line up in silence as they entered the chapel for the ceremony. However, Mount Sackville was part of Blanchardstown parish at the time. The priest who said the Mass had to travel by horseback from Porterstown. Sometimes this made it difficult to establish the actual arrival time of the priest and the Sisters were aware of the need for the girls to have breakfast, after Mass, in order to begin classes punctually.

Mount Sackville was quite self-sufficient in the 1940's. Most of the vegetables, fruit and meat were produced on the grounds. Where the main car park is now, there was a huge orchard. In front of the convent there was a row of glasshouses. Large fields surrounded the convent, where crops such as potatoes were grown and cattle, sheep and domestic fowl were reared.

The National School was located near the chapel. The laundry and some of the Sisters' sleeping quarters were located on the site of the present-day school reception and Career's Office. The present National School was built in 1954 and later extended, with the addition of a Concert Hall and two classrooms.

Mount Sackville employed farmers and caretakers to tend the farm and of course many sisters helped in the labour intensive tasks.

Sister Colm recalls two men who worked in Mount Sackville. John Brannigan and Pat Murphy, and how Pat's melodious singing voice floated in the evening air as he sat milking the cows. The Sisters often paused to listen to him. She also remembers Michael Little's father living in the gate lodge, when he was appointed caretaker of Mount Sackville, and Michael, as a little boy of six or seven, moving in with him.

Sister Marie de Lourdes Moran

Sr. Marie de Lourdes is a native of Salthill, Co. Galway. She spent six years as a boarder in Mount Sackville in the 1940s. She joined the Cluny Sisters after her Leaving Certificate. She spent time on the missions in the West Indies, particularly in St. Lucia and Trinidad, before returning to Mount Sackville in the late 1970s. Sr Marie de Lourdes remembers with fondness her days as a boarder.

"In the 1940's, classrooms were along the chapel corridor, where the present sisters' dining room is located. Just off the chapel corridor was a large wooden building where Musicals were performed, drill classes were held and evening recreation [usually ballroom dancing] took place. This building was eventually replaced by the Sisters' infirmary. The school uniform was changed during the 1940s. Originally navy blue, the present colour, royal blue, was then adopted. Pupils had the option of a cream or mustard blouse. The year of the change-over, pupils, anxious to show off the new uniform, walked to Stewart's Hospital in Palmerstown on St. Patrick's Day."

Sr. Marie de Lourde's time as a boarder coincided with the war years. In May 1941 pupils had their annual retreat and were advised as was customary, to make the retreat 'as if it was their last'. Shortly afterwards, on the night of the 31st of May 1941, the Luftwaffe bombed Dublin, killing thirty four people. The damage was most severe in the North Strand. However some bombs fell in the Phoenix Park, not far from the school. Sister Marie de Lourdes remembers hearing the noise and seeing the flashes as the bombs fell.

In the midst of panic the pupils seemed more interested in seeing the nuns in their night attire, without their all-encompassing veils, than they were worried about the prospect of annihilation.

Until the present library was built, Sr. Marie de Lourdes worked as a Librarian in the old library. She was conscious of the fact that she worked in the room that had been her dormitory in the 40's. She continues to give music lessons in Mount Sackville."

Students in the 1940's, among them Sr. Marie de Lourdes Moran, Sr. Emmanuel McNamara (deceased),
Sr. Cecilia Kelly, Sr. Maria McGrath, Sr. Joan Ryan, Sr. Ann Therese Murray, Sr. Frances Mary Keegan (deceased),
Sr. Mary Doyle and Sr. Eucharia McCloone.

Mount Sackville in the 1950's

Mount Sackville in the 1950's

The First Foreign Students

The first foreign students began to arrive in the 1950's. This was through the encouragement of Sister Germaine Moses, the Bursar. Through careful planning, she encouraged students from France, Spain, Mexico and many other overseas missions to come here. Being a good Bursar, she made sure their fees included their return journey, in the event of an urgent need to go home. She also ensured good homes for the girls, so that they had guardians to care for them during holiday time. Foreign students from all five continents made up a large percentage of the boarding school until its closure in 1996. Mount Sackville continues to welcome students from all over the world and from every religious background. It has at present among its day pupils, students from Africa, the Middle East and Asia, whose families are working and living in Ireland.

Annette Andrews

Annette (Cusack) Andrews was a boarder in Mount Sackville for five years in the early fifties. Her mother, aunts and uncle (Michael) had been students before her and she was followed by three younger sisters and her young brother, Paddy. A small school at this stage, there were only seven others in her Leaving Certificate Class. Annette Bird, Imelda Reilly, (Sister Agnes), Olive Plunkett, Pat Cunningham, Jean Clarke and the twin day pupils,Olive and Doreen Keyes.

Annette is currently Chairperson of the Board of Senior Examiners with the Royal Irish Academy of Music. At the same time she continues to play and gives small private recitals from time to time. In 2002 she made her public debut in the John Field Room of the National Concert Hall.

Annette remembers with fondness her days in Mount Sackville:

"When I was eleven I left my home village of Ballyjamesduff, Co.Cavan for Mount Sackville. It was September 1950. I was excited and scared.I had always known I would be going. No Secondary School in Ballyjamesduff and no school transport gave my parents no choice in the matter. Also, it was always going to be Mount Sackville as my mother, her sisters and brother had been there before me.

I made a lot of friends eventually but my saviour on the first evening was Annette Bird. Although she was going to be in my class, she had already been there for six years as her mother had died when she was very young. She knew the ropes and helped me with the business of making my bed (a first for me) and letting me know all the do's and don'ts. Annette and I are still good friends.

Apart from my periodic bouts of loneliness (no weekends home for me) I enjoyed my time in Boarding School. Of course I didn't like getting up at 6.45am to go to Mass and often tried to feign illness for another hour in bed. We gave out about the food, but I have to admit now that it was quite good.

Mount Sackville was quite a liberal school. Personally, I got huge encouragement in Music. I had a wonderful teacher, Mother Berchmans, who was probably the only nun with whom I never got into trouble. Over the years I gradually gave up subjects I didn't like (top of the list was Domestic Science), and was allowed to spend the time practising, eventually on the grand piano in the big parlour, which was quite a concession.

One of the people I remember most was Lena. Small and plump with white hair cut short and wearing a large sparkling white apron, her domain was the corridor between the entrance hall and the school. Here was Lena's kitchen, the phone booth, the priest's parlour and two other parlours. It was her domain and she ruled the roost always knowing who was coming and going. Whenever I was in trouble I would retreat to Lena's Kitchen. She had been there in my mother's time so she always looked after me. I would get tea, sympathy and a bun!

In my final year Mount Sackville had become a small and intimate school with only about fifty pupils, far different from the modern thriving school it is today. I am proud to be a past pupil of such an excellent school."

Frances Fagan (née Bird)

Frances Fagan was a pupil in Mount Sackville in the 1950's. The following is a little reminiscence of her time in school:

"There was no secondary school in Kilcock in the early 1900s so the Presentation nuns who ran the Primary school there for over 80 years set up a Continuation Class for girls to attend until they reached the legal school leaving age. I spent two years in the 50's in that class in the 'Bungalow' a lovely summer house where the older girls learned all aspects of household management - cookery, knitting, sewing etc, and office duties - book keeping, typing, and filing . There was a big mail order store, a thriving bakery and a large garage in Kilcock in those years, so girls went straight from school to work in these premises - usually until they married or went abroad. At the age of 14 (a bit late) my parents decided to send me on to Secondary Education and as an aunt-in-law had attended Mount Sackville years earlier, it was their obvious choice for me.

I had the unusual privilege of being both boarder and day pupil in Mount Sackville. There were very few day pupils in those years - just a few girls who came up from the Junior School run by Mother Columbanus. There were many girls from abroad, Trinidad, Spain (Lourdes and Violet Artinano - cousins) India (Amy Dwasack) and Wattina Peninctesa from the East. I enrolled in Mount Sackville in September 1956, and was greeted by the ever faithful Lena and Mother Gabriel, the Superior. Her relative, Ronnie Delaney, had just won an Olympic Gold Medal for Ireland, so sport was very high on the agenda. I got my first taste of Hockey that year, having only played Camogie at home. We went out to the Phoenix Park every Wednesday afternoon to practise and my father would arrive on his moped with a fresh apple tart and other treats for me. I loved Wednesdays and looked forward to his arrival. Tennis was ongoing with two hard courts in front of the convent - I had never played on a hard court before and really enjoyed it.

I was enrolled in third year. It was all so different from primary school. I had so many teachers. Miss McCarrick and the art teacher, Miss Smyth, were the only lay teachers at that time. Mothers Thomas, Dominic, Agnes, Celine and Louisa are the nuns I remember most and I will never forget Mother Alexis for quietly ejecting me from her Latin Class.

I never settled down as a boarder, even though my life was full of new and exciting subjects. I loved music and was involved in the orchestra under Mother Columbus. I played the Viola for the first time and loved it. We held several recitals. We had a brilliant choir too, conducted by Mother Eugene. I can still remember our rendition of 'Come to the Fair' - my first encounter with harmony. To this day I sing Alto with my local church choir and am a member of Kildare and Leighlin Diocesan Choir directed by Fr. Liam Lawton. I took piano lessons from Mother Eugene but she didn't appreciate my playing chopsticks up in the cells when I should have been practising my pieces, so she politely told me that there was no point in wasting my parent's hard earned money. (Another ejection)!! As I was an only daughter and the youngest of the family I couldn't bear being away from home. At the end of my first year my father and Mother Gabriel decided I would never settle down but they agreed I should try again, this time as a day pupil. In September 1957 I returned to third year again. (I must not have studied too hard the first year)!! I had to leave home at 7.30am, get the bus to Chapelizod, walk up the hill and arrive in school in time for Mass each morning. I stayed after school until 4.30pm. This was a good opportunity to get some homework done before the walk down the hill again for the bus which left Dublin at 5pm and had me home by 6pm. It was a long day and tough going in winter, through wind, hail and snow but I was much happier!! I sat my Inter Cert in 1958 with Imelda Bonass, Mary Bowles, Joan Cullen, Mary Cusack, Linda Hamill, Brenda Hartnett, Rita Lynch, Ailis Massey, Aileen Murray, Yvonne MacDonald, Catherine McDonald, Breda

McElligott, June McNally, Christina O'Callaghan, Helen O'Reilly, Pauline Parsons and Mary Rochford. WHERE ARE THEY NOW ??? In September 1959 I went on to Commercial College in Dublin, joined the ESB in 1960 and remained there until my marriage in 1965. That's another story!!!"

Amy Dwasack & Maida Cooney during the Tennis Final in Mount Sackville, 1958

Sister Conleth pictured in 1959 in the grounds of Mount Sackville with John & Bridget Noonan, grand-parents of Emma Dunne (4th Year), 2004

The Mount Sackville Orchestra pictured in the Old Hall in 1957

*Mother Celine,
Mount Sackville
1956*

*Lourdes & Violetta
Artinand, Mount
Sackville 1958*

*Fifth Year Day Pupils
in 1956
From left: Rita Dunne,
Marie O'Connor (RIP),
Clare Molloy,
Patricia McLoughlin*

Carmel Fox and Mabeth Murray at the chapel door of Mount Sackville, 1958

5th & 6th Year Students in 1956

Frances Bird, Mary Giblin, Maura Whelan, Pat McCaffrey and Peter Mount Sackville, 1958

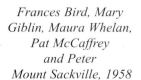

Mount Sackville in the 1960's

To commemorate the centenary of the arrival of the Cluny order in Ireland, the congregation published a centenary souvenir brochure and centenary celebrations were held on the 16th, 17th and 18th of October, 1960. In the centenary brochure, the Very Reverend Mother Marie of Saint John, Superior General at that time wrote the following:

> *"The grain of seed sown in the soil of the Archdiocese of Dublin on the 12th of December 1860 by the arrival of Mother Callixte Pichet and two other Sisters from Paris has developed into a tree which extends its branches over the world. The Irish Sisters of Saint Joseph of Cluny are to be found in the five continents."*

In fact, Mount Sackville had become a fertile soil and during the first one hundred years of the establishment of the order in Ireland, over a thousand girls had become members of the congregation. The boarding school, established by Mother Pichet in 1864, continued to thrive. To facilitate the growing needs of the students and to celebrate the centenary, the first big expansion took place in 1960, when a new block was added. The 'Centenary Block' was built with money collected by Sisters and parents knocking on doors all over Dublin selling tickets and twisting the arms of friends and relatives to buy bricks. This new extension consisted of the Assembly Hall, a number of classrooms, the 'brown corridor' and an Art room. The extension was designed by Mr. P. Maloney B.Arch., M.R.I.A.J. (Messrs. O'Connor and Aylward, architects) and was constructed by Hugh O'Neill and Company, contractors. Centenary celebrations got under way with the visit to the school by the Most Rev. John Charles McQuaid D.D. Archbishop of Dublin. The Apostolic Nuncio presided at Solemn High Mass in the Convent Chapel. The Kimmage Choir sang the Mass. Among the many other guests was the French Ambassador to Ireland Mons. Jacques Paris.

No school year in Mount Sackville would be complete without the production of one of the leading operas in the Assembly Hall. *"Eire, The Handmaid of the Eucharist"* was beautifully performed by the pupils, and greatly appreciated by all who saw it.

"Eire, the Handmaid of the Eucharist", performed in the New Assembly Hall in 1960

The Dining Room in 1960 - Eilish Massey, June McNally, Joan Cullen, Mary Curley, Sheila Kelly, Mart Hartnett & Brenda O'Brien

Mother Gabriel Delaney, Superior of Mount Sackville
greeting pupils returning from their summer holidays in 1960

From left: Sr. Elizabeth Smith, Sr. Aloysius O'Reilly and past-pupil Eilish
Galligan pictured at the main door in Mount Sackville in the 1960's

Christine Dwyer Hickey

Christine is an award-winning novelist and short-story writer. Twice winner of the 'Listowel Writers' Week Short Story Competition'. She was also a prize winner in the prestigious 'Observer/Penguin Short Story Competition'. Her trilogy, *"The Dancer, The Gambler and the Gate Maker"*, has received critical acclaim. Christine has also written a screenplay, adapted from her own short story, for the film *'No Better Man'* starring Niall Tobin. Her recent novel *'Tatty'* has proved to be a huge success.

Christine remembers the following about her time as a boarder in Mount Sackville:

"I came to board at Mount Sackville Junior School in the late nineteen sixties. My previous school had been a large National School with forty-odd girls squeezed into one room and where we all more or less resembled each other with our pasty, Irish freckly faces. The first thing I noticed when I walked into a classroom in Mount Sackville was the variety of faces,although it seems absurd now that we live in a multi-cultural society but then, in 1969 to a small child I might as well have come to board on the moon. There were pupils from Africa, India, Malaysia ,Mexico, Hong Kong and as if that level of exoticism wasn't enough to knock me off my feet, there were also BOYS in the classrooms,including one rather splendid specimen who sported a matching shirt and tie in paisley print and also a large ring which he used to stamp the family insignia on the hot red wax that sealed his out-going letters. I have to say that Mount Sackville Junior School was the making of me. Up to this I had been an introvert and always had a slight sense of shame that somehow I had done something wrong or was about to do so at any given moment. In my old school Irish, Sums and the ability to turn the heel of a sock seemed to be all that mattered. Art classes were non-existant and Drama consisted of elocution,a stiff-gobbed affair along the 'how-now-brown-cow' lines. Now, in Mount Sackville, suddenly the world opened out to me under the guidance of Sister Dominic and Miss Reid, probably two of the best teachers I've ever had. I learned that self-expression was nothing to be ashamed of and that learning didn't necessarily have to be painful. I tried to recapture the school and the way it was then in my novel "Tatty", I hope I succeeded. I am always delighted when anyone who has been to Mount Sackville and that has read "Tatty", has recognised the corridors and stairways, the smells and the atmosphere, the dormitories where we all slept like nested mice. Yesterday, I spoke to my friend, Anita, in

Italy, Ruth, in Galway and received an email from Concilia in India. These are girls I met and with whom I lived with, all those years ago in Mount Sackville. These girls have become women and have remained my friends. That says it all really."

Paul Maher

Paul Maher and his family from Clonee, Co.Meath, have a long association with Mount Sackville. The following are his memories of the school:

"Mount Sackville was the 'Education Centre' for me and my six siblings. My sister, Rosemarie commenced her Primary Education there in 1950, followed by David, Gervaise, Bernice, Patricia, myself and lastly Bryan. Bryan's class was the last class of boys to complete sixth class in the school. I remember when our parents went away on holidays we were all deposited as boarders in Mount Sackville for the duration of their vacation. During those times I served Mass and remember serving at Mother Norbert's funeral Mass. Lena looked after us in her kitchen every evening as our Dad would collect us at 6.45 pm on his way home from work. Lena spoilt us with tea and cake.
My class had only four boys in it, Michael Sullivan, Oscar O'Herlihy, Peter Cosgrave and myself. It gave us great experience in dealing with the female species for later years. Virginia Kerr was one of our classmates and I am sure Sister Peter Cronin would be very proud of her today. The Maher Boys all went to Secondary School in Castleknock College and the girls continued in Mount Sackville. I have three daughters all of whom are graduates of the school. Congratulations to Mount Sackville on its 140th anniversary and I wish them many more successful years."

Monica Mc Gill

Monica attended Mount Sackville in the mid 1960's and is the mother of Jenny, a present sixth year student. Monica kindly provided the following reflections on her days as a boarder:

"How could it be that long ago? September 1965? I resist the apprehension of admitting that it's now part of a previous millennium.
The idea of going to Mount Sackville Boarding School - a frightening and

exhilarating thought! Would it be like St. Trinian's films, all jolly hockey sticks, and midnight feasts?

The experience of boarding school turned out completely different from my expectations. It was better in some respects and worse in others. The cubicles were small but adequate. The beds were surprisingly comfortable. The three main dorms seemed huge and I didn't expect that our Mistress of Studies would be sleeping in the first dorm on the left. At meal times, Mother Eugene would come to the "Ref", ring the handbell for silence and then would announce anything of importance: the basketball third team won (or lost) their match, the new list of chores for Saturdays had been put up on the noticeboard and would everyone please make absolutely sure that their cubicles were clean and neat, and ready for inspection on Saturday "and Mother Alexis would be grateful if all library books could be returned promptly." "Black marks will be awarded for those who failed". We were each put into one of four houses in the school. Towards the end of the term, at a general assembly, we had to stand in line in our houses. All the teaching nuns and the few lay teachers we had back then sat on the stage looking down at us.Once our unnerving delinquency had been described to the assembly,the house with the lowest black marks were given a Gala Tea in the "Ref", while the rest had to partake in cleaning duties around the school.

Imagine the shock of coming back to school one September and discovering that nuns had ankles!! They'd shortened their skirts to mid-calf, cast off their head-gear and in this post Vatican era changed their titles to 'Sister.' They had always called each other 'Soeur' but we'd always called them 'Mother' up to then. It was a big change at the time.

In sixth year we decided we'd have to remedy a certain situation: we had never had a midnight feast! The date was set. The secret arrangements were made. Each girl was in charge of providing an essential item. I was to bring roast chicken. Others brought bread, butter, mixed salads, biscuits, tayto crisps, club orange, coca-cola and chocolates. We smuggled knives, forks and a big metal jug, out of the "Ref" My grandmother sent me in, not one roast chicken but a boxful of them. She was good at things like that. Everyone in the class assembled at the top of the grand staircase at twelve midnight on the dot, each with her forbidden bounty. Stifling giggles, we made our way in velvet darkness down the stairs and past the statue of St. Joseph, and the portrait of our order's foundress. All was grand, until Mary dropped the metal jug half-way down the stairs. It contained all the cutlery.

In the vast chasm of the house and the stillness of the night, Rip Van Winkle would have known something was afoot. We all raced to the stage in the Assembly Hall, and pulled across the heavy blue curtains. We stood absolutely still, hoping, looking at each other. Not a sound. When our hearts had returned to their natural positions, we dared to start in. But we forgot: nuns glide when they walk, and Sister Eugene wore slippers at night. She could easily have held a doctorate in gliding. It was the shortest midnight feast in the history of any boarding school. In the gliding department none of us were cut out to be nuns!

So what can I say to the cohort of pupils in Mount Sackville today? Enjoy it. Rarely again will you meet in your lives the kind of dedicated mentors you know there."

Dr Patrick Hillery Visits Mount Sackville

Dr Patrick Hillery, then Minister for Education, visited the school on the 17th October, 1960. He delivered the following address:

"Soilse, a Thiarnaí, agus a dhaoine uaisle eile, idir chléir agus tuaith.

I think I speak on behalf of you all in congratulating the Sisters of St. Joseph of Cluny on the attainment of their centenary in Ireland, in conveying to them our appreciation of the great work they have done both here and abroad during that period and, thirdly, in thanking them for the very gracious reception we have been privileged to enjoy at their hands today.

No few words of mine would express the extent of their success in their great mission. Perhaps the best way of bringing it home is to glance at the list of countries where since the Congregation was founded in 1807 by Blessed Anne-Marie Javouhey, it has established itself, namely, Ireland, England, Scotland, France, Spain, Portugal, Italy, Switzerland, Africa, India, West Indies, the U.S.A, Canada, South America, New Zealand, Australia, the Fiji Islands, the Society Islands, the Marguesas Islands, the Cook Islands, the Seychelles, Madeira and the Azores. This roll of names, with many of the foundations manned, as one may quite properly put it, by our Irish girls and women, leaves one almost breathless - literally as well as figuratively!

Ireland had the good fortune to receive the Sisters in 1860 at a time when there was almost no provision here for the secondary education of girls. The country's response was immediate, and by the end of the first year, twenty three Irish girls had entered the Dublin Novitiate. Since then the Irish Province has never looked back. Mount Sackville, the school in which we stand, was established in 1864, the Mount Sackville National School in 1890, Ferbane Secondary School in 1896, Mount Sackville Boys' Preparatory School in 1906 and in 1914 the Sisters undertook teaching in Ferbane National School.

Such an occasion as this gives rise to reflection. That so many centenaries of Orders and Congregations are being celebrated here at present must strike one as remarkable. One hundred years ago it would not have occurred to many that a small poor country, stricken by famine and to all appearances politically and socially moribund, had any part to play in world affairs. Humanly speaking, that forecast would be the only possible one. But in the ashes of the Famine collapse there was still an ember which was to blow into flame in many directions. It is not, I believe, in the heart of man to despair utterly, and indeed despair in the spiritual realm would be a kind of contradiction in terms. Nevertheless, it is to the everlasting credit of such Congregations as this that in that time of depression, poverty and misery, they were the first to cast away doubts that the vital spark was still alive in our people. Only the stoutest of hearts could have provided the truly apostolic zeal that was then needed to co-operate with the grace of God, as we now see has been done so fruitfully.

Hardly any part of the world to which there is free access is without its band of Irish nuns and other religious and in that wonderful effort the Sisters of St. Joseph of Cluny are in the forefront.

But all this is not so strange, if we reflect also that this mission of religious and educational zeal is in the direct line of our traditions. From the sixth to the tenth century Irish religious foundations were flung in a belt across the centre of Europe, right in the path of the invading barbarian hordes. The task of Christianising and civilising these must have looked formidable, but as far as one may judge from the literary remains, those Irish 'exiles for Christ', as they were happy to call themselves, seem to have taken it in their stride. Today it is not Europe alone which is at stake, but the mind of man throughout the world, and once again the Irish missionaries are seen quietly, but efficiently devoting their lives as a matter of course to the noblest cause that is open to a human being, the spiritual and temporal assistance of his less fortunate neighbour.

To the Sisters of St. Joseph of Cluny and to all our other far-flung mission-aries I think I can say that, while their personal sacrifice is Ireland's loss, it would be small-minded of us to grudge the rest of the world its gain. It is part of the spirit of your Congregation to shun laudation and publicity, but we, here at home, do appreciate that you are 'the salt of the earth' which adds the savour to our country's place among the nations.

Go mairidh sibh fada buan agus nár lagai Dia síbh."

Reception Room, Mount Sackville 1960
*Included in the photograph are Rev. Mother Gabriel,
Most Rev. Dr. Moloney, C.S.Sp., Bishop of Bathurst, West Africa,
Very Rev. Mother General Marie of St. John,
His Excellency, The Apostolic Nuncio to Ireland, Most Rev. Dr. Byrne,
Most Rev. Dr. McGee, Bishop of Galloway, Scotland,
Rev. Mother Gemma, Irish Provincial Superior,
Dr. Phelim Coldwell, C.R.P., Lord Abbot of Kilnacrott,
Rev. Michael O'Carroll, C.S.Sp., D.D.*

Centenary Celebrations at Mount Sackville, 1960
Mr. Kavanagh, Surveyor, Mr. R. Guy, O'Connor & Aylward Architects,
Dr. P. Hillary, Minister for Education, Mr. T. Rafferty, The Secretary,
Dept. of Education, Mr. J.V. Tierney, Consulting Engineer.

Centenary Celebrations at Mount Sackville, 1960
His Grace, Most Rev. J.C. McQuaid, D.D., Archbishop of Dublin

Centenary Celebrations at Mount Sackville, 1960
The children pictured with the Very Rev. General Mother Marie of St. John

Mount Sackville in the 1970's, 80's & 90's

The 1970's witnessed further expansion of the school buildings: 1972 saw the addition of classrooms at the back of the Assembly Hall, while a Gymnasium, classrooms and Science laboratories were added in 1976.

Pupils at the gates of Mount Sackville, c1970

The next big phase of construction and change took place in the 1990's. Following the closure of the Junior School in 1996 and the expansion of the Secondary School to cater for the ever-increasing demand for places, the classrooms of the old Junior School and the Sisters' Laundry became St. Joseph's Block in the Secondary School. A modern Art Studio was developed on the first floor in 1993 along with a Computer Room, offices and a new Home Economics Kitchen.

> *"The old order changeth, yielding place to new,*
> *and God fulfils himself*
> *in many ways"*
>
> [Tennyson]

The 1990's was to prove to be a very historic decade in Mount Sackville. 1992 saw the appointment of the first lay principal, Mrs. Marian McCaughley. Marian arrived in Mount Sackville in 1974 as a Higher Diploma student, having completed her BA degree in U.C.D. She joined the staff teaching History and Geography in 1975 and was appointed as Principal in 1992. Marian has brought considerable leadership skills, enthusiasm and encouragement to this position with her dedication and commitment. She, along with a team of committed teachers has made Mount Sackville what it is today.

1994 a saw the introduction of the Transition Year Programme into the school. This was part of an overall national development in education at the time. Transition year, a year bridging the Junior Certificate and Leaving Certificate allows the students to experience a wide range of educational opportunities including Personal Development, Mini Company, Community Work.

1996 was to witness an end of an era in Mount Sackville with the closure of not only the Junior School but also of the boarding school which was synonymous with Mount Sackville since its foundation in 1864. Perhaps as a *"sign of the times"* and with the deep regret of parents and pupils, Mount Sackville Boarding School closed its doors for the last time in June 1996.

Sixth year students and staff, 1969-70

Marion Mc Keone

Marion is the U.S. correspondent with the Sunday Tribune and is a past pupil of Mount Sackville. She kindly submitted her memories of her school days.

"Rebels. Reprobates. Delinquents. Teachers love to tell students that there has never been a class as badly behaved, ill-disciplined or ill-mannered. The class of 1980 heard it loud and often, but then we were often loud and privately we conceded that Sr. Agnes may have had a point.

We reached our teens at a time of enormous cultural change in Ireland. Punk rock and its attendant filled our heads. Keeping control of our number must have been akin to herding cats.

Of our year I remember irrepressible high spirits, an inexhaustible supply of pranks that must have driven the staff to distraction, impromptu hockey games in the classroom where bloodlust triumphed over skill every time. Like most teenagers we were obsessed with music; there were endless battles over who would dominate the creaky old stereo. For a while "The Clash" reigned but more often than not Michael Jackson won the day. General George Patten would have been impressed by the covert operations and battle tactics we employed to ensure that punk ruled - at least in the common room.

There was always mischief and laughter and a non-stop quest for more of the same but somehow the teachers managed to corral our high spirits into high standards and academic achievement.

The influence of teachers has often been stated but can not be overstated. Mary McDonald's love of English and of learning for its own sake, rather than simply as a means to accumulating the requisite number of points. Tony O'Flynn's determination that every pupil in his class would realise her potential pushed many of our year to standards we would never have otherwise reached. Nor was his dedication limited to the curriculum. The Debating Society he founded didn't just provide an outlet for those of us with a penchant for speaking our minds. It taught us also the importance of thinking before speaking and of respecting the opinions of our opponents.

We were an unruly bunch; that the teaching staff succeeded in importing any knowledge in our heads - filled as they were with Michael Jackson and Sid Vicious and how we would wrangle tickets to see "The Ramones" on a Thursday night - was in itself a major achievement. That they also instilled values that would transcend the classroom and our teenage years and serve as a ballast for what life brought was arguably the greater achievement.

Much of the teaching was by example; Sr. Agnes' patience and humour-- even when taxed to its limits by our antics--and Sr. Angela's fairness and integrity taught us lessons that were not forgotten. Twenty-four years later, while many of us have ended up many thousands of miles from where we started, the friendships we forged and the lessons we learned are still with us. Our conversations are still peppered with "Do you remember the time...?". We do with amusement and an appreciation that has grown with the years."

Graduation Mass, 1977

Sixth year students 1970 - 71

Front Row: Rosemary Kelly, Helena Hardiman, Gabrielle Croke, Clare Coleman, Ruth McCann, Jean Igoe, Marian Neary & Sandra Farrell.

Middle Row: Mary McHugh, Terry Morag, Olivia Renehan, Nicola Quinsey, Anna McGee, Wendy DeFruitas, Sheila Rodgers, Virginia Kerr, Barbara Cleary, Miriam Kelly.

Back Row: Gráinne Dillon, Susan Shannon, Maureen Ruigrok, Gabrielle McCallion, Hilary Quinn, Jennifer Mullen, Anne-Marie Flanagan

Sixth year students 1972-73

Back Row: Judith Gavin, Rachel Rhatigan, Indo Tauko, Noelle Murphy, Phil Mooney, Margo Hurley, Terry Prudin, Jane Hughes, Bernice Nolan, Sheila Kelly.

Middle Row: Dee McGarry, Lopa Guha, Susan Williams, Fiona Watson, Claire Gibson, Mary Joe Moore, Sheila McCallion.

Front Row: Maureen Phelan, Sandra Mullan, Catherine Keane, Marie O'Gara, Noeleen Curley, Lynn Bisseisar, Isolde Croke.

Catherine Walsh (née Keane) is currently a member of the teaching staff at Mount Sacville School

84

The Teaching Staff in 1974/75

Back Row: Sr. Consilio, John McHugh, Tony O'Flynn, Tony Robinson, Dick O'Sullivan, Robert Molloy, Terry Dolan.
Middle Row: Jim Quinlan, Sr. Eugene, Maeve Gilligan, Pauline O'Callaghan, Sr. Agnes, Noreen Deveraux, Carmel Kavanagh, Sr. Angela, Rhoda Haywood-Jones
Front Row: Sr. Alexis, Mary MacDonald, Maeve O'Neill, Marian Murray, Santiago Sia

The end of the Boarding School Era

Ms. Margaret Dee, Mistress of the Boarders at the time and at present a member of the teaching staff gave the following insight into her memories of the boarding school:

"In the end is the beginning..

Standing on the stairs with nothing but the dust-filled columns of light around me, I can still hear the voices of young girls, generations of which have resonated around this beautiful staircase. There is silence now - a silence which is both sad and hopeful. The sadness comes with the closure of the Boarding School, which was what Mount Sackville was at its inception. The hope is for the generations of women who have passed down this 'staircase' as pupils and who are now the people of our modern Ireland, highly educated women in all walks of life.

Being a boarder for a short time, and having previously worked in the running of boarding schools, I was both happy and apprehensive when asked by Sr. Agnes to look after the Mount Sackville Boarding facility in 1990. The Sisters of St. Joseph of Cluny, like many other female religious orders in the '90's were in the process of change and there were no Sisters available to do the work at that time. I asked her what life was like in the boarding school: what kind of spirit pervaded. Her description of a place of faith, where young girls were 'at home', and were for five days of the week dedicated to study and the pursuit of things which would allow them to grow as people, was so like what I had experienced in my own schooldays that I accepted the challenge. For me, boarding school education has always been a rounded approach to growing up, not suited to all, but for those who participate in it to the full, an experience which one never forgets. We have many testimonies in this latter half of the century to the nightmare quality of this experience for some. We also have the silent testimony of the thousands of women for whom this experience was 'the best time in their lives'.

This was evident in the number of parents I met, some of whom I had been at school with myself, who wanted their daughters to have the same chances in life they had; others perceived it to be the best, without the experience. All wanted their children to have something special. So what is so special about this form of education? To be given, at the start of one's life, the ability to be independent, self-disciplined and generous has to be something special and these three 'gifts' are, I believe, what a boarding school education has to offer. If we look at the women of this century, our grandmothers, mothers, our-selves and our daughters, we cannot but be aware of the wealth of personal spirit, ability, talent, and faith, which has been the driving force in this nation of ours. Whether it be as wives and mothers, as politicians, as bankers, as nurses and doctors, as missionaries and teachers, as assistants in all walks of life, as carers and innovators, they have been the silent, and not-so-silent, voices of Christ, of Christianity, of humanity, not only in Ireland, but all over the world. These are the women who benefited from a boarding school educational system, run by a body of women who spent their lives giving to young people a 'duty of care' such as has, as yet, to be equalled in our modern times.

I write today in praise of these women whose contribution to modern education, and modern Ireland, is of great importance. All things must of their nature change if they are to be strong, vibrant and life-giving. Education is no different in this respect. But, in the process, of change we often forget the best of what is past. As this century passes, let us not forget those who created the present so that there could be a future.

I am grateful to the St. Joseph of Cluny Order, and Sr. Agnes, their Irish Provincial Superior in particular, for allowing me participate in a way of life, alas now all but defunct in its present form, out of which I came and to which I hope to have given a little in my four years in Mount Sackville. In that time we had two young women from Australia who, as my assistants, gave much and received much. For Julie Ford and Genevieve Tomkin, the Irish experience is something they will draw from for the rest of their lives. And everyone's thanks must go to Bernie Clarke, who will never be forgotten for her constant care of all of us over very many years.

When you ask those who have been in a boarding school what they remember, the first thing they will speak of are the friendships they made. The bonds forged in the initial loneliness, the subsequent sisterly care, and the shared delight and comfort of a secure existence, are never forgotten or broken. The chapel, a focal point in the daily life of all, spoke of the presence of Christ, of his command to love, and the daily morning and evening prayer as 'a family', are all things which we remember, and are supports in the hard times in life. We remember especially the Christmases: the Mass, the dinner, Christ Kindel, the decorations and the carols around the crib. Then there were end-of-term parties, the special occasions when sixth years met with the lay staff, who also contributed to their lives with their academic and personal help as well as study supervision. The outings at, and before Christmas to various places as year groups, again with the help of lay-staff, showed them another side of their teachers! One could go on for ever! But what about the academics? The hours of study which these young women choose to do over and above those they had to do, speaks for itself to those of us who bear witness to it.

The good times and the bad times, the joys and the rows, the personal pain and the shared laughter are all things I now cherish as I remember the people who passed down these stairs during my time in the boarding school. It is a privilege, not granted to all, to be able, for a few short years, to be in loco parentis to other people's children, all of whom I hold in my heart with deep affection. It only remains for me to thank them for allowing me to be a part of their lives. Now it is time for me, too, to pass down this staircase with my memories out into the day school area and to bring, with the rest of my colleagues, the best of what is past to what we will become in the future."

Margaret Dee

Sr. Rosaleen Cummins, gave her insight into her role as a Supervisor of Boarders:

"The supervision of boarders was an assignment I accepted fully aware of what I would encounter. I looked forward to what I regarded as a special mission among those girls. So, I stepped in with an open heart and a listening ear, catering to their needs. As the weeks and months went by, I grew close to the group and we got on well together on the whole. It was normal that there were the occasions when individuals, or the group, had to be 'called to order', and the inevitable unpleasant moments followed... But taking a stand and being firm with young people is appreciated by them in the end.

It is now past tense and it is rewarding to note that when these same young ladies now drop in to see me, their comments reveal that they retain happy and positive memories of their boarding school days - they can even enjoy reminiscing on how they got into trouble and on the punishments meted out to them!

As you read these lines, girls, remember that I, too, have very good memories of you. I wish you all the best and I ask the Lord to Bless you all your days."

Sr. Rosaleen Cummins

Ms. Dee, Mistress of Boarders, Sister Enda Hanley, Sister Maura Ronan, Sister Marie de Lourdes and Sister Philomena Kenny at the celebration commemorating the closure of the Boarding School

Pupils Remember

"An important part of Mount Sackville came to an end with the closure of the Boarding School. The news meant the sad departure of many of our friends, leaving the remaining thirteen of us to stay for the final year. Under the careful supervision of Sr. Rosaleen we all agreed to make the year one to remember. After all, it did mean we could be historical figures of the future.

And what a year it was! From late night chats and fashion shows to watching "Friends" and "ER" religiously every week we became a small family. Around our ever decreasing dinner table, we exchanged fights, jokes and long discussions on the important issues in our lives....men (or the lack of them in many cases).

We have all agreed on the wonderful experience it has been for all of us and the unique effect it has had on us as individuals. It is a shame that this era has ended, but I am happy to have shared in the life it offered. I have to thank Ms. Dee and Sr. Rosaleen for their encouragement and help throughout the years. I hope that the friendships I have made will last a lifetime and I will carry my memories as a Boarder wherever I go."

Sonya Toner

What Boarding Meant To Me

"When I was first told that I was going to boarding school, I couldn't believe it. Our mother had always threatened that if we didn't behave and help out, she would send us to boarding school. Of course, my sister and I never believed it would actually happen, so when it did, we were terrified and were convinced it would be dreadful. This was my worst nightmare, but I was wrong, and I'm glad to say that the pre-conception with which I entered Mount Sackville was proven to be completely unfounded. In fact, boarding here is probably one of the best things that has ever happened to me. I have learned how to adapt to other people and have made friends that I know I will keep forever. Of course, we were all shocked and upset at the closure of the boarding school, but I will always cherish the fond memories of a wonderful three years."

Claire Miller

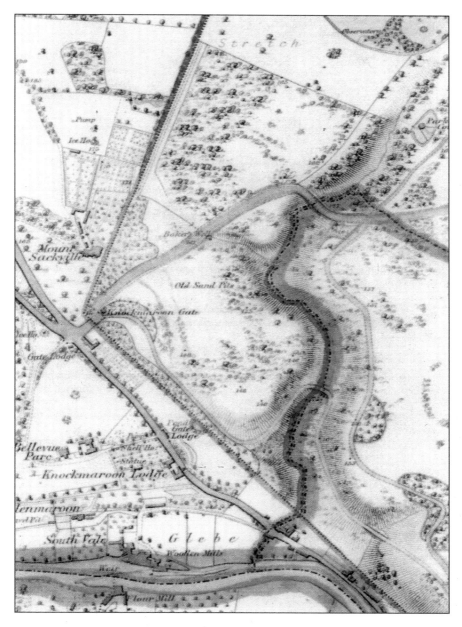

Map showing the estate of Mount Sackville, 1837
Permission of Ordnance Survey Ireland© Permit No MP 008404

Aerial view of Mount Sackville in the 1980s.

Chapel at Mount Sackville pre Vatican II

Chapel at Mount Sackville, 2004

Students Hazel Morrin O'Rourke and Sarah Flood present the President with a bouquet of flowers.

President Mary McAleese addresses the school on the occasion of the 140th Anniversary.

The Board of Management, 2004 pictured with the President during her visit to Mount Sackville to mark the 140th Anniversary Celebrations

Back Row: Mrs. E.Ward, Sr. Maeve Guinan, Mr. F.Casey, Mr.T.Dolan, Mrs. E. Higgins, Mr. F. Connolly, Mrs. N. Corbett

Front Row: Mrs. M. McCaughley, the President Mrs. Mary McAleese and Sr. Monica Sheehan

Mrs Nuala Corbett, Board of Management, Mrs. Marian McCaughley, School Principal,
Sr Maeve Guinan, Provincial of the Sisters of St. Joseph of Cluny,
Mary Hanafin, Minister for Education and Sr. Monica Sheehan,
Chairperson of the Board of Management pictured at Mount Sackville's
140th Anniversary Celebrations at the Royal Hospital, Kilmainham in 2004

Teaching Staff, 2004

Graduation Class, 2004

A group of Sixth Year Students during the last years of the boarding school

Our Days at Mount Sackville Junior School

"Our days at Mount Sackville Junior School were wonderful. Whether we were there from Junior Infants all the way up to sixth class, or were only there for a term, it was a lovely place to be.

The first teacher we had was a young nun, a novice, called Sr. Rowena. She rode a moped. She taught us for one year only, in Junior Infants, as the closure of the Junior School was then imminent.

91

The next teachers to leave were Miss O'Catháin, Mrs. Doyle, and also Sr. Magdalen, our Head-Mistress. We had Sr. Magadalen in first class and she will always be remembered. After Sister left, Miss Brennan took over as Head-Mistress. Miss Brennan taught us in High Infants, Fourth Class and Fifth Class. When Miss Brennan left the school, Miss Reid, the only teacher remaining, became our principal.

We were always encouraged to do well in our studies and constantly strived for excellence in various aspects of the curriculum, such as badges for 'Girl of the Week', or, when we were small, a sticker for 'ten out of ten' in a spelling test. We had supervised study after school, and Miss Reid would help us do our homework, and she guided us in our studies in Fifth and Sixth Class and helped us prepare for secondary school.

When we were younger, we had a party and a video every Christmas. We also had a Mission Drive where we raised money for the missions by selling toys and books that we didn't want, but which were in good condition. We held raffles with baskets filled with goodies such as soaps or sweets.

We also had extra subjects such as French and Computers. Miss Barrington taught us Speech and Drama. We sometimes entered for Feiseanna and occasionally won medals. Mrs. Taaffe coached us in Hockey while Mr. Bradshaw taught us tennis.

Mass was celebrated for us on holy occasions, at the beginning and end of every year. The saddest Mass ever held in the school was the last one. After Communion two girls removed the Junior School flag from behind the altar. A few hankies were pulled out of handbags to wipe away the tears of mothers who had sent their daughters there from the beginning. After Mass, the doors of the Junior School were closed forever."

Jasita Lalloo

The Teaching Staff in 1983

T. Robinson, R. O'Sullivan, R. Molloy, Sr. Marie-Thérèse, M. McCaughley, M. McDonald, C. Crotty,
J. McHugh, Sr. Angela.

T. Dolan, M. O'Neill, M. Lavin, A. Thornton, P. O'Callaghan.
Sr. Eugene, A. Cummins, Sr. Una, M. McNulty, A. Flanagan.
T. Lewis, Sr. Gabriel, Sr. Consilio, Sr. Agnes, Sr. Alexis, Sr. Assumpta, Sr. Peter.

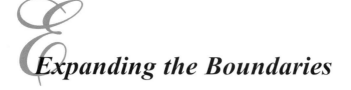

Expanding the Boundaries

In 1998 two big dormitories were converted into accommodation for the Sisters. What had been the teachers dining-room was converted into offices, one for the matron of the nursing home. The chapel was decorated in the same year and the old infirmary was demolished.

Preparation began in 1999 for the development of a new school library which was completed in April, 2003. This has been of enormous benefit to the school, providing students with access to a wide range of references, internet access, video library etc. Our librarian, the ever-enthusiastic and dedicated Ms. Aileen Ivory, is always willing to assist and encourage the girls in the use of the library facilities. In the convent, work began on a new infirmary. The building was registered by the Eastern Health Board on 26th of April, 2001.

Perhaps the greatest expansion of Mount Sackville Secondary School was launched in 2000 by the newly formed Board of Management, with the encouragement of Principal Mrs. Marian McCaughley and the guidance of Mr. Niall O'Sullivan. A project called *'Expanding the Boundaries of Learning'* got under way. A major strategic review to assess the future direction of Mount Sackville was undertaken and a number of needs were identified. The committee began a fund-raising campaign and through the generosity of parents, local businesses and past pupils, Mount Sackville has successfully completed phase one of this expansion project.

The new facilities included:

A new Language Laboratory which has been instrumental in students improving their skills in European languages. The satellite dishes enable students to view live French, German and Italian programmes.

Ms. Flanagan demonstates how to use the new Language Laboratory

A new flood-lit Astro Turf pitch, has been of great benefit to students. The pitch was instrumental in assisting our team to reach the final of the Leinster Schools' Junior Cup for the first time, the year following its installation.

The new all-weather Astro-Turf Pitch, opened in 2003

The new Library

The new Ceramics facility, opened in 2003

The new Art Room, opened in 1996

A Computer Room update offers students the opportunity to take the European Computer Driving Licence (ECDL)

A newly installed kiln in the Craft Room extended our students' range of craft options.

In the increased car parking area, forty-three new car spaces were added between the National School and the existing hockey area.

These above facilities enable Mount Sackville to continue the pursuit of excellence in Academics, Music, Art and Sport which has been the tradition of the school for the past 140 years and has been instrumental in developing Mount Sackville into one of the premier schools in Dublin.

The official opening of the new facilities took place on the 29th of March, 2003. The facilities were blessed by Fr. Sam Clyne and opened by Mr. Brian Lenihan TD, Minister of State at the Department of Health and Children. The ceremony was attended by Sr. Maeve Guinan, Provincial Leader of the St. Joseph of Cluny Sisters, members of the Board of Management including, Sister Monica Sheehan Chairperson of the Board, parents, students, teachers and staff.

In her address, Sr. Maeve acknowledged the hard work and dedication of Mrs. Marian McCaughley, assisted by Mary Higgins and other staff which made this project possible. She ended her address with the following:

> *George Bernard Shaw "saw life as a sort of splendid torch that I've got to hold up for the moment and I want to make it burn as brightly as possible before passing it on to future generations". "You Mrs. McCaughley, staff, Board and parents of Mount Sackville have done that and we thank you".*

Fr. Sam Clyne blessing the new facilities

Mr. Brian Lenihan, T.D., Minister of State at the Dept. of Health & Children, Sr. Maeve Guinan, Provincial of the order of Saint Joseph of Cluny and Mrs. Marian McCaughley at the Official Opening of the new facilities in 2003

Dr. Mary Candron presents the Parents' Assocation Award to its first recipient Ms. Stephanie Davy on the occasion of the opening of the new pitch in 2003

Official Opening of the new facilities in 2003

Front Row: Sr. Maeve Guinan, Provincial, Mrs. Marian McCaughley, Principal, Mr. Brian Lenihan, T.D., Sr. Monica Sheehan, Chairperson.

Back Row: Mr. Richard O'Sullivan, Mr. Terry Dolan, Ms. Mary Higgins, Mr. Frank Casey, Mrs. Nuala Corbett, Mr. Frank Connolly, Fr. Sam Clyne, Mr. Tony Robinson

Music in Mount Sackville

From its foundation Mount Sackville considered Music essential to the curriculum.

In 1910 there were fifty girls in the Special Choir, individuals excelled themselves in Music and Singing. The Orchestra comprised fifteen violins, three Cellos, two violas, a drum, a flute and a piano. Music continued to be an essential component of a Mount Sackville education.

Many names are associated with Music down the years, those of Sr. Berchmans, and Sr. Colm Keane among others. Mount Sackville made a musical impact on the National stage with the advent of Sr. Eugene McCabe, Sr. Peter Cronin and Mrs. Aideen Lane.

Sister Eugene McCabe

Sr. Eugene (Maureen McCabe) was born in Glasgow but the family moved to Ireland when Maureen was eight. She was educated at Loreto Convent, Cavan. From a very young age she travelled to Loreto Abbey, Rathfarnham for harp lessons; her early giftedness was richly fulfilled all through her life. Sr. Eugene studied piano, organ and harp. She obtained a degree in Musicianship in U.C.D, having previously achieved an A.R.I.A.M in piano and harp. She arrived in Mount Sackville in the 50's and gave thirty-nine years of devoted service to the Music Department in Mount Sackville. Her great love was the harp and she made Mount Sackville synonymous with excellence in this instrument. This is a quotation from a letter of sympathy from one of her former pupils after her death, *"When I was in Mount Sackville Special Choir and Musicianship classes were the only classes I looked forward to....the love Sr. Eugene had for music was a love she passed on to so many pupils, and this is a tribute to her."*

Sister Peter Cronin

Josephine had previously considered the thought of entering a convent. But it was one night in the Capital Theatre that she made her decision. Now she had to break the news to Gustav Sacher, the man who could have opened for her the gates of fame, riches, and worldwide knowledge in the operatic world. We allow Sr. Peter to say it: *"he told me that if it was what I really wanted, then it should be done, but the great and all perfect God would be my constant audience therefore, my singing had to be as near perfection as possible"*.

In January, 1952, the tiny seven-stone lady went for interview to the Cluny Novitiate in Ferbane. She struggled with the thought for another five months and then on the feast of the Sacred Heart, June, 1952, she joined the Congregation in Ferbane.

Sister Peter is at present in the St. Joseph of Cluny community in Portlaw, Co. Waterford. Her contribution to Mount Sackville is awesome. Many of her past pupils have achieved much success both at home and abroad.

Sister Peter Cronin with past pupil Virginia Kerr at Mount Sackville's 140th Anniversary celebrations at the Royal Hospital, Kilmainham, 23rd November, 2004

Mrs Aideen Lane

Mrs. Aideen Lane is a graduate of U.C.C. and Dublin City University. Before taking up a teaching position in Mount Sackville in 1987 she was a soloist with many choral societies around Ireland. She sang with the Dublin Grand Opera Society, Irish National Opera and at the Wexford Opera Festival. She also performed on R.T.E. and B.B.C.

Aideen started singing lessons with Sr. Peter Cronin in Mount Sackville in 1985. In 1987, Sr. Peter convinced her to take Choir one day a week. Her one day a week became two and eventually she took a full-time position. In 1992 the first Junior Certificate class sat their exam in Music and the first Leaving Certificate class took their exam in 1995. Every year since then, there has been an exam class.

From the choirs' first participation in Feis Ceoil in 1988, where they won second prize, choirs in Mount Sackville have gone from strength to strength. It took a few years for Special Choir to establish itself as lunch time practices were not too popular. Now they are an integral part of school life. Aideen recalls the many performances and achievements of her students to date. She recalls in particular a beautiful radio Mass in 1989 with Sr. Eugene McCabe playing the organ and Helen Gilsensan singing the psalm. She also remembers a visit to the school by the composer, John Buckley, where the Choir learned and performed *"The Eagle"* all in one day!

1991 saw the Special Choir perform on B.B.C. 2's *"Songs of Praise"* from St. Patrick's Cathedral, Dublin. In 1996 a third year Music class went to Grafton Street to perform *"Brachan Lom"* on NBC T.V.'s *"Today"* programme. The Special Choir performed in a *Christmas Concert* in Luttrellstown Castle in 2001 and made an appearance in *The Point Depot* with *Russell Watson* in 2002. One of the most memorable ventures was *"The Island Journey"* Concerts which took place in *The Waterfront*, Belfast and the National Concert Hall, Dublin. 1990 witnessed the production of *"The Gondoliers"*, which was produced by Mr. Maurice O'Sullivan. Since then an operetta has been produced every year. One of Aideen's personal highlights is the *Annual Christmas Charity Concert*, performed in the Convent Chapel each year.

While all choirs in Mount Sackville have distinguished themselves in competition, the Special Choir has achieved great success. The Choir competed in *The Cork International Choral Festival* in 2004 and were placed second.

The Special Choir of 1991 won the competition that year. 1991 proved to be an extremely successful year for Mount Sackville. Among the prizes achieved were the *'John Cunningham Trophy For Best Choir'* and the *'Sean O'Riada Prize.'*

Aideen has many pleasant memories of music-making in Mount Sackville but she will never forget the sheer beauty of the Choir's singing of *Micheal Head's "Ave Maria"* in the National Concert Hall in 1998.

Aideen Lane assisted by her dedicated music staff, Mrs. Nuala Staines and Ms. Sharon Carty continues to cultivate the tradition of music in Mount Sackville.

The 2004 Orchestra with their teacher Ms. Sharon Carty

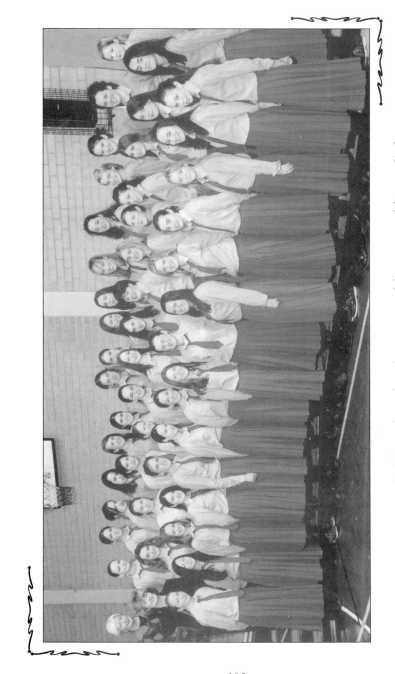

A Special Choir performed on the occasion of the opening of the new facilities. Pictured with their music teachers Mrs. Aideen Lane & Mrs. Nuala Staines

Physical Education in Mount Sackville

Ann O'Connor
P.E. Teacher & Past Pupil of the school ·

Mr. Myles, our coach, took us for PE drill and Hockey every Wednesday afternoon. Both were held in the Assembly Hall.

Sr. Eugene was responsible for the extra curricular activities.

Hockey: Instruction was normally held on the front lawn and occasionally in the Phoenix Park,which ajoins the school. Even in bad weather we were encouraged to take regular exercise by going for brisk walks in our *'teddy bear coats and berets'*. Matches were arranged against Dominicans Wicklow, Loreto Foxrock, and St. Joseph of Cluny, Ferbane.

Basketball was also becoming popular, as was tennis. A complete PE programme was introduced in 1976. A new sports' hall was erected at the same time providing us with an indoor basketball court, four badminton courts and an indoor tennis court. There were six outdoor tennis courts and three outdoor basketball courts.

Mount Sackville soon entered their first hockey Leinster league team in competition. We were fortunate to have the Phoenix Hockey club pitch available to us for our practice sessions and the girls were always very enthusiastic.

1978 saw the arrival of our All-Weather Hockey pitch and we entered a team in the Leinster League. Our PE Department continued to expand and in 2002 our facilities were further updated with the construction of an Astro-Turf pitch. This pitch can accommodate a variety of seasonal sports, including tennis, cricket and hockey.

The Physical Education Department has developed so much in the last number of years because of the dedication of the PE staff. We now have a variety of sports on offer, basketball, hockey, badminton, tennis, self-defence, horse-riding, gymnastics, canoeing, aerobics, football, yoga, volleyball, cricket and swimming. Teams in most activities have been entered in leagues. This year two of our canoeists took part in the Liffey Descent. We also host the Mount Sackville School Horse Show each year.

Patricia Campbell, Ann Flood (now Ms. O'Connor), Aideen Barks &
Marie Connellan in 1967

The first ever Leinster League Hockey Match played by Mount Sackville in
1975 (Phoenix Park Hockey pitch)

Senior A Hockey Team in 2004

Back Row, from left: Patricia Crummey, Ruth Maloney, Riona Molloy, Laura Meehan, Ciara Foley, Lydia O'Connor, Emily Lyons.
Front Row from left: Kate Hurley, Andrea Davy, Aislinn Freeman, Julianne Brogan, Roz O'Connell, Aoibhinn Garrihy

Under 14 Division 3, Winners of Dublin Schools' Badminton.
They secured second place in the Leinster Final, 2004
From left: Sally Wong, Claire Murray, Karen Carty and Elsa Hogan-O'Regan

Art in Mount Sackville

The standard of Art work in the school has always been very high. Sister Alexis Murphy was a keen artist and inspired an interest among her students. She taught in Mount Sackville in the 1960's and 1970's. The drive and ambition of the students has ensured their continued success both in state exams and in regional and national competitions. In 1996, Elaine Cowley won the Telecom Eireann Design-A-Call Card Competition. Elaine was chosen from forty thousand entrants. Her teacher was Mrs.Christine Crotty whose talent and love for Art has encouraged all her students. Christine herself designed a pictorial map of the ancient 'Walls of Dublin' which was presented to Bill Clinton, former President of The U.S.A. during his visit to Ireland in 1995. The Art Department under the auspices of Ms. Trish Lanigan and recently appointed Ms. Alice Brady continue the pursuit of excellence in this subject.

Facilities are constantly improving. The arrival of a Kiln, Potter's wheel and Plug Mill are the latest additions. A purpose-built Art room to rival any design studio, Craft room and Television Communications' facilities have given the students the option to explore a wide range of media,giving them valuable experience when pursuing future areas of study.

Emma Brannigan, Overall winner of the Texaco Childrens' Art Competition in 2001

Elaine Cowley with her prize-winning design in 1996

Other Cluny Second Level Schools in Ireland

Ferbane

In 1896 a small group of Sisters travelled from Mount Sackville to Ferbane in the Irish Midlands and founded a Secondary School there with a small boarding section attached.

With the advent of Free Second Level Education in the late 1960s, the school population expanded rapidly and it was decided to amalgamate with the local diocesan boys' school, to enhance the range of facilities for all the students in the town and surrounding catchment area.

Over the past decade, with the closure of the Ferbane ESB Power Station and the subsequent scaling down of Bord Na Mona in the area, the population has decreased. In September 2004 the school again amalgamated to ensure continued top class education in the district.

St. Joseph's / St. Saran's and Ferbane Community College now form Gallen Community School, Ferbane. The Sisters of Cluny feel proud and privileged to continue as joint trustees of this school.

Killiney

St. Joseph of Cluny Secondary School, Killiney was founded from Mount Sackville in 1956.

The original house is set in acres of rolling farmland. It belonged to the Belton family and before that to the Blacker Douglas family - owners of the B and I shipping line. It has a magnificent view of Dun Laoghaire Harbour on one side and Killiney Hill on the other.

A handsome secondary school was erected on the site and this has been extended tastefully on a number of occasions.

There are at present about four hundred and fifty students in the school and there are plans afoot to build more classrooms and a library.

The school has established a strong academic and holistic tradition, characteristic of Cluny schools worldwide.

Teachers & Staff

Mount Sackville has among its teaching staff many past-pupils, including; Mrs. Ann O'Connor, Ms. Mary Begley, Mrs. Catherine Walsh, Ms. Tina Lewis, Ms. Louise Boylan, Ms. Olga Owens, Ms. Trish Mulcahy, Ms. Julie-Ann Somers and Ms.Niamh O'Sullivan. It also has a number of long-standing members of staff including, Mr. Tony Robinson, now deputy principal, Ms. Maeve O'Neill, Mr. Tony O'Flynn, Mr. John McHugh, Mr. Dick O'Sullivan and Mr. Terry Dolan.

In order to establish how the school has changed in recent years, a number of Transition Year students compiled a questionnaire and carried out interviews with a number of staff.

I wish to thank my colleagues for kindly agreeing to be interviewed and for sharing their experiences of change with us.

Mary Begley

Mary Begley who teaches French and German recalls that most of today's facilities existed when she was a student. The Library and Art Room are part of the new extensions to the school; these were formerly in the convent section. The closure of the Private Junior School allowed for much greater accommodation and additional classrooms. The music rooms are now located in the school section; they were previously in the convent as was 'Sick Bay' or 'Infirmary'. It was there that as *"timid first year pupils"* they all queued for their Rubella vaccinations. Transition Year was introduced in the mid 90's and it offers a wide variety of modules such as Personal Development, Mini Company, Film Production - all exceptionally interesting. Classical Studies has also been introduced as an option at senior level. Computer Studies leading to the ECDL is very popular, too. The system of *'Tutors and Deans'* taking responsibility for different year groups was only in its infancy during her time in Mount Sackville.

Terry Dolan

Mr. Terry Dolan, Transition Year Co-Ordinator and teacher of History, Maths and Computers recalls his first impressions on arriving in Mount Sackville. Having successfully secured a teaching position in the school and having been presented with his timetable and text books for the forthcoming year (neatly wrapped for him in wallpaper) he began his first Civics class in the "prefabs". However, this proved to be a little disastrous! The text book was devoid of illustrations and dry as dust. While he was attempting to clarify the topic, one pupil, looking a little perplexed announced *"Sir, you use awful big words"*. To add to the confusion, there was a bomb scare later that same day and the remaining classes had to be conducted on the lawn. Despite this, Terry did return to school the following day and is at present a valued member of our teaching staff.

Tina Lewis

Ms Tina Lewis teaches French and German. When she was a student the teaching staff was much smaller in relation to today's number. More subjects are offered now but one area remains strongly represented, Modern Languages. Originally French (compulsory), German, Spanish and Latin were taught. Physics, Economics, Classics and Italian have been introduced into the curriculum over the years.

John McHugh

Mr. John McHugh, a teacher of Geography and Maths, was the second male teacher to join the Staff with Mr. O'Sullivan. He notes that the changes that have come about over the past three decades reflect the changes in Irish society generally as post primary education has become more accessible to all. Up to 1967 the voluntary Catholic fee paying boarding school was a dominant force in Irish education and Mount Sackville was one of these establishments. There are other members of Staff who arrived in the two years following his arrival and they

Ms Lena Mescal

are still 'going strong' namely Mr. Tony Robinson, now Deputy Principal, Miss Maeve O'Neill and Mr. Terry Dolan. Mr. McHugh has vivid memories of Miss Lena Mescal, who came from Co. Clare and worked as Receptionist in the convent. 'Lena's kitchen' was a meeting point for the Staff. Lena, a dear friend of the Sisters was the 'hub of community life', had a great warmth and understanding of people. She was an honorary member of the Sisters of St. Joseph of Cluny. She passed to her eternal reward in 1985. May she rest in peace.

Tony O'Flynn

Mr. Tony O'Flynn teaches Business and Accounting. He told us that he applied for a permanent position in May 1974 and was very happy when he was told a week later that he had been accepted. He said that when he was shown around the school after his interview by Sr. Angela, he was impressed by what he saw and in particular by the Convent Chapel, which he describes as a very special place. He pointed out, as many others have done, that structurally the school has changed. The Secondary School is now totally separate from the convent. The most notable difference for him is the cessation of the vibrant boarding school in 1996. Apart from the Sisters who taught in the school, so many others took responsibility for different areas which served both the convent and the school. Tony says that the contribution of the Sisters to Mount Sackville's success is immeasurable. They were totally committed at all times. he regrets the fact that the Sisters are no longer involved in education in Mount Sackville because he believes that Sisters have a huge impact and influence on students in their earlier years. Religious vocations are on the decline in Ireland and this he feels is a great loss for students.

Dick O'Sullivan

Mr. Dick O'Sullivan, recently retired Vice Principal and teacher of Maths, remembers that when he joined the Staff over thirty-five years ago he was the first male teacher in the school. He mentioned the many students who came from all over the world; some of these students were nineteen or twenty and saw Mount Sackville as 'a finishing school' similar to finishing schools in Switzerland. There was a farm attached to Mount Sackville, and both the boarders and the convent enjoyed the produce.

Catherine Walsh

Mrs. Catherine Walsh, a past pupil, who teaches Business and Accounting says that in her school days exams were taken very seriously but fortunately the awful points system did not exist. As mentioned before Music, Harp Choir and Sports were given high priority in the school programme and, as is the case today, many competitions were won. Among the overseas students there was a special group from Mexico, who did not attend the regular classes but were here to learn English. Each year there was a concert where all the different nationalities were attired in their native costumes and performed a variety of national dance. Students came from Mexico, Canada, U.S.A. Thailand, Africa, Spain, Seychelles and India.

Mary Higgins

Mary Higgins is a past pupil of Mount Sackville and a relative of the late Sister Kevin Hope. Mary was appointed as the first lay Bursar in May 1993. She has been a careful and prudent steward of school finances over the years.

Michael Little

Michael Little's family have been associated with Mount Sackville since the 1940's, when his father, the late Henry Little was employed by the Sisters. Michael and his brother Tommy together with Edward Kavanagh contribute enormously to the day to day running of the school at present. Carol Kearney, Michael's niece and a member of the secretarial staff is the third generation of Littles to work in Mount Sackville.

Principals and Provincial Superiors at Mount Sackville

Provincial Superiors of Mount Sackville

1860 - 1888
Sr. Callixte Pichet

1888 - 1931
Sr. Gabriel Horner

1931 - 1936
Sr. Gabriel Mary Gallagher

1936 - 1949
Sr. Stanislaus Forde

1942 - 1946
Sr. Paul Molloy

1958 - 1967
Sr. Gemma Duffy

1967 - 1975
Sr. Bernadette Reilly

1975 - 1983
Sr. Stanislaus Byrne

1983 - 1989
Sr. Morag Collins
First English speaking
Mother General

1989 - 1998
Sr. Agnes Reilly

1998 -
Sr. Maeve Guinan

Principals

Formerly, three people were connected with running the school :-

- Superior "Manager" signed papers.
- Mistress of Studies organised classes, etc. and dealt with the Department of Education
- Mistress of Discipline.

Names connected with post of Mistress of Studies were~:
Sr. Paul Molloy, Sr. Teresa Kelly, Sr. Thomas Fox,
Sr. Ursula Garvey........finally Sr. Nora Kenny.
Sr. Gabriel Delaney, who had been Superior, was moved to another community in 1962 : Sr. Nora Kenny then became principal.

Principals from 1962 Onwards

- 1962 - 1967   :   Sr. Nora Kenny
- 1967 - 1975   :   Sr. Angela O'Grady
- 1975 - 1989   :   Sr. Agnes Reilly
- 1989 -   1992   :   Sr. Celine O'Byrne
- 1992 -   :   Mrs Marian McCaughley

The superior of Mount Sackville continued to be "Manager" of the secondary school up to the mid-nineties. 1998 saw the appointment of the first ever Board of Management to the school.

Sister Nora Kenny

Sister Nora completed her secondary education in King's Inns Street School, Dublin. Later she attended U.C.D. where she secured a B.A. Degree,a H.D.E. and a Diploma in Cathechetics. At Maynooth N.U.I. she obtained a Diploma in Theology. Having taught in Mount Sackville for several years she was appointed Principal in 1962, a post she held for five years, known then as Sr. Agnes Kenny.

Sister Angela O' Grady

Sister Angela attended primary and secondary school at Presentation Convent, Terenure. She obtained a B.A. Degree and a H.D.E. at U.C.D. She later studied at Milltown Institute and Trinity, where she was conferred with a B.D. Degree. Her teaching career began in Killiney. In 1967 she was appointed Principal in Mount Sackville, a post she held for eight years.

Sister Agnes Reilly

Sister Agnes attended Blackrock Primary School and completed secondary education in Mount Sackville. She attended Sion Hill College and later U.C.D., where she obtained a B.Sc. Degree and H.D.E.. She held posts in Ferbane, and Stafford and served as Principal of Mount Sackville from 1975 to 1989. She also served as Provincial of the British Isles and is currently in charge of the Nursing Home in Woodlock, Portlaw, Co. Waterford.

Sister Celine O'Byrne

Sister Celine's primary education began in Dublin and was completed in Offaly. She attended Moate Secondary School and completed her secondary

 education at St. Joseph's Ferbane. Later she attended U.C.D. where she obtained a B.A. Degree, a H.D.E., a Diploma in Catechetics and a certificate in School Librarianship. She later attended Lancaster University, where she secured a D.A.S.E. in counselling. Having held posts as teacher and principal in both Killiney and Rosary College, Crumlin,she was appointed Principal of Mount Sackville in 1989, a post she held for three years.

Mrs. Marian Mc Caughley

Marian Mc Caughley (Murray) was born in Scotland and educated there for most of her primary education. She attended secondary school in St. Dominics' College, Cabra and then studied History, Geography and Philosophy in U.C.D. for a B.A. degree. In 1974 she came to Mount Sackville for teaching practice as part of her Higher Diploma in Education and joined the staff in 1975. Later she attended N.U.I., Maynooth and T.C.D. achieving a Diploma in Education Management and a M.Sc. in Education Administration. Marian is married to Brendan and has four children; Elaine and Claire, who are past pupils of Mount Sackville, and Gordon and Michael. Having taught in Mount Sackville for seventeen years Marian became the first lay principal of the school in 1992.

Mount Sackville 2004

A Student's Perspective
Gillian O'Halloran - 5th Year Student

Mount Sackville has changed dramatically since its founding in 1864, from the facilities to the subjects. Today's average school week is a world apart from what it used to be. There is a constant buzz of six hundred students, all clad in blue, to be felt all day everyday. There are always clusters of girls talking about what they did over the weekend or who the latest love interest is!

Our school has given us great friends, with whom we can share these great experiences. However, Mount Sackville has enabled its students to expand their horizons in a variety of ways. We have been introduced to all sorts of sports, art, drama, science, languages, charities, debating, music, film, dancing and even mini-company among other things.

We have excelled in our chosen areas too. Each year the school produces athletes who fill up our trophy cases with numerous awards from all sorts of sports including badminton, tennis, basketball, athletics and, of course, hockey. We have won the award for best overall school at the Santry Leinster Schools' Athletics competition for the last three years in succession.

Many music students participate in multiple competitions and feiseanna throughout the year and they always perform to the highest of standards, regularly receiving prestigious awards! The Special Choir and Senior Madrigal Singing Group compete in Feis Ceoil and the Cork International Choral Festival every year. We have won in both categories of both competitions in the last few years and have always received outstanding marks.

The school is host to many different charities including the St. Vincent de

Paul (SVP), Respect, Amnesty International and Focus On Romania (F.O.R.) SVP and Respect are continually organising inter-schools fundraising events. Amnesty has students representing the country in the Amnesty Youth Organisation! F.O.R. recently visited Romania for the first time with a small group of senior students who spent a week going to the different orphanages that they have helped over the years.

Debating is an ever-popular activity in Mount Sackville with in-house debates taking part during lunch times up to five days a week with students from second to sixth year taking part while first years participate in workshops organised and run by the very active Debating Society. And, as in many other activities, Mount Sackville achieves an impressive standard of competitive inter-schools debating with senior students taking part in the U.C.D., L&H Mace, the Trinity Mace, the Concern Debating Competition, the Mental Health Public Speaking Competition, the Aoife Begley Memorial Debating Competition, the Leinster Schools Debating Competition, and in recent years, the Try-outs for the All Ireland Team!

We enjoy (for the most part) our classes with our very dedicated teachers who, not only are great at teaching, but are also selfless in giving their free time to assist us with some of our extra curricular activities (as mentioned above). Our teachers are encouraging and approachable. No girl is ever afraid to express her opinion...even if she knows that a heated class discussion will ensue!

Our school is an enjoyable place to be, despite what we may tell you after being dragged out of bed on a wet January Monday morning! Our Prefects, Sports' Captains, Class Captains, Debating Secretaries and Student Forum Representatives and teachers all ensure that every need of every student and all of her talents are catered for, to ensure that we continue to enjoy the remainder of our precious school days.

Even though the school has changed dramatically in the last 140 years, our ethos has remained the same through the years:

FIDES   *FAITH*

SPES   *HOPE*

CARITAS   *CHARITY*

140 Years Celebrated

To commemorate the 140th anniversary, President Mrs.Mary Mc Aleese visited the school in May 2004. In her address to the students and staff ,she commended the Sisters of Saint Joseph of Cluny for their contribution to education in Ireland. She also paid tribute to the teachers and students of Mount Sackville. To mark the occasion of the anniversary,the school celebrated Mass, with the other Cluny Communities in Ireland, namely, St. Joseph's Ferbane and Killiney. A past pupil, Fr. Dermot Lane, celebrated the Mass on the 11th of November, 2004, the date on which Blessed Anne-Marie Javouhey consecrated herself to God.

As a further mark of celebration, a Gala Concert was held in the Royal Hospital Kilmainham on the 23rd November, with pieces performed by past pupils Virginia Kerr, Annette Andrews, Teresa and Mary O'Donnell, our own *"Special Choir"*, the past pupils choir and orchestra. Special guests included Mary Hanafin, T.D., Minister for Education, Maura Clancy, Assistant Chief Inspector, Department of Education and Science, Sister Maeve Guinan, Provincial of the Sisters of Saint Joseph of Cluny and many Cluny Sisters.

The Minister for Education spoke to the choirs after the performance and commended them on their talents. In her address she said that *"providing the opportunity for you to express your talents and develop them is the mark of an excellent school"*. The concert was enjoyed by all who attended.

Much has been written about Anne-Marie Javouhey, and her own letters are quoted and reproduced over and over. However Albert Schweitzer, that other great servant of Africa best expresses the secret of her courage and serenity when he says *"the only ones who will be really happy are those who have sought and found a way to serve"*. Perhaps this is as fitting a memorial as any to this truly extraordinary woman. May the work begun by Blessed Anne-Marie in 1807 continue in the hearts and minds of future generations.

*President Mary McAleese greets Sr. Enda Hanley, Sr. Bernadette McGarry and
Sr. Theophane Halpin during her visit to commemorate the 140th Anniversary*

Teaching Staff at Mount Sackville 2004 / 05

Marian McCaughley, Principal
Tony Robinson, Deputy Principal

Sr. Bridget
Grainne Boland
Phil Boyle
Alice Brady
Peter Burke
Sharon Carty
Margaret Dee
Mary Delaney
Alex Dwyer
Alacoque Flanagan
Eileen Higgins
Monica Keating
Claire Kilroy
Patricia Lanigan
Noreen Lynch
Marianne Magrane
Evelyn Monahan
Gerard Murphy
Ann O'Connor
Gerard O'Leary
Dick O'Sullivan
Bernadette Prendiville
Julie-Ann Somers
Ann Thornton

Mary Begley
Louise Boylan
Nessa Bourke
Sarah Bryant
Angela Carty
Therese Courtney
Gerry Deegan
Terry Dolan
Dioreann Fallon
Mairead Griffin
Anne Hillan
Aisling Kelly
Aideen Lane
Tina Lewis
John McHugh
Ann Meade
Patricia Mulcahy
Maura Murphy
Tony O'Flynn
Maeve O'Neill
Olga Owens
Jennifer Simmons
Nuala Staines
Catherine Walsh

Range of Subjects available to each student from 1933-1986, Leaving Certificate:

Irish, English, Latin, French, Spanish, Italian, German

Arithmetic, Algebra, Geometry, Chemistry, Physics, Physiology

History, Geography, Drawing, Domestic Science, Commerce, Business, Art, Botany, Accounting

Subjects available to students from 1986-2004, Leaving Certificate:

Irish, English, French, German, Italian.

Maths, Biology, History, Geography, Chemistry.

Accounting, Economics, Applied Maths, Music.

Classical Studies, Home Economics, Art, Physics.

Note:
In 1996 only fifty students took the Leaving Certificate.
This was due to the introduction of Transition Year in 1994.

It is important to realise that in the years immediately following the establishment of Mount Sackville, many students who attended the school, never actually sat a public exam. This was true of all secondary schools in the Ireland of the time.

Students who completed their Leaving Certificate in Mount Sackville
1933-2004

YEAR	Students	
1933	M. Brennan	C. Kenny
	M. Harbowne	M. Morrissey
1935	Barbara Finneran	Maureen Bowles
1936	Sheila Renehan	Peggie Cavey
	Ita Delaney	Kay Kearney
	Maeve O'Daly	
1937	Mary Murphy	Marion Geoghegan
	Marion O'Reilly	Eileen Malone
1938	Patricia Murphy	Kathleen Kennelly
	Nuala Mahon	
1939	Kathleen Lane	Annie Butler
	Mary Murphy	Maeve McKenna
	Mairead O'Connell	Mary Moore
1940	Brigie Keenan	Betty Maguire
1941	M. O'Reilly	Bernadette Cavey
	Marie O'Brien	Joan Kearney
	Kathleen Hayes	
1942	Teresa Keenan	Ethna Moran
1943	Dolores McKenna	Bernie Ryan
	Frances Scally	Phyllis Stephenson
	Betty Moran	Barbara Savage
	Bea Cloonan	Kitty Fagan
	Agnes Darcy	

YEAR	Students	
1944	Kathleen Flanagan Maureen Little Annie McLoone	Pauline Gerety Mary McLoughlin
1945	Theresa Hayes Nuala O'Hely	Frances McLaughlin Marie Wall
1946	Eileen Kelly Brigid Markey Veronica O'Brien	Brigid Hoban Mary McCusker Charlotte Ward
1947	Angela Lannion Madeleine McLoughlin	Nan Macanlay Ethna Murphy
1948	M. Byrne A. Leavy B.O'Callaghan	T. Fleming E. Murphy B. Egan
1949	B. Bolger E. Mc Kenna	A. Callan T. O'Sullivan
1950	K. Daly B. Loughlin S. Sweeney	M. Kelleher M. O'Byrne
1951	E. Galligan Sr. Emmaurd	J. St. Leger
1952	Betty Byrne Susie Danielle Mary Kilgarrif Ann Moran Maura Smyth	Nora Corriston Mary Hamilton Clare Little Ann O'Gorman

YEAR	Students	
1953	Claire Daniels M. Graham	Fidelma Lennon
1954	Mary Burke Deirdre Kelly Bernadette McGarry	Maureen Healy Teresa Loughlin Maura O'Hely
1955	Annette Bird Annette Cusack Imelda Reilly	Pat Connerton Olive Plunkett Jean Clark
1956	Eileen Crehan Noreen Joyce	Terry Connerton Yvonne Kelly
1957	Rita Dunne Helen Raftery	Ursula Kelly Wattana Phinainitisatna
1958	Rose Clark Mary Larkin Pat McCaffrey Anne McKeown Nuala Prendergast	Pauline Crosbie Vera McArdle Mary McDermott Denise Prendergast Amy Dworzak
1959	Christina Connolly Freda Fenton Bernie Mc Elligott Angela O'Donovan Cathy Kelly	Ann Dardis Nessa Healy Judith Ryle Maureen Sala
1960	Catherine Coleman Carmel Fox Pat Mc Ardle Pauline Ruane Noreen Tuohy Patricia Punnett	Una Connolly Siobháin Kelly Gillian O'Donovan Christina Sweeney Maura Whelan

YEAR	Students	
1961	Patricia Casey	Joan Cullen
	Mary Cusack	Mary Harte
	Sheila Kelly	Ailís Massey
	June Mc Nally	Brenda O'Brien
	Johanna Koom	
1962	Maura Clancy	Mary Curley
	Catherine McDermott	Bridget O'Keeffe
	Mary Sheridan	Mary Sweeney
	Mary Moran	Patricia Whelan
	Noreen Hastings	Elizabeth Smith
1963	Frances Bowles	Jon Casey
	Joan Collins	Josephine Delahunty
	Mary Flahive	Frances Gannon
	Ursula Gray	Sheila Hyland
	Mary Lawlor	Aleyoque Martin
	Margaret O'Donoghue	Maeve O'Farrell
	Antoinette Ronan	Kathleen Steadman
	Maureen Walsh	Mary White
1964	Brenda Banim	Maria Bonanate
	Mary Carroll	Clare Cusack
	Ann Fox	Caroline Gavin
	Imelda Halpin	Brenda Hughes
	Bridie Moran	Gemma Murphy
	Eleanor O'Donoghue	Kathleen Reid
	Margaret Smith	Charlotte Sweeney
	Marion Willoughby	Helen Delahunty
	Ada Duorzak	Fanny Margai
	Brenda Punnett	Helen St. Hill

YEAR	Students	
1965	Mona Crowe	Irene Farrell
	Eileen Fields	Valerie Goff
	Rosemarie Maher	Helena Mc Keown
	Stephanie Martin	Mary O'Connor
	Catherine O'Neill	Caroline Guinan
	Ada Swarzak	Regina Rogers Wright
1966	Tena Banim	Aideen Barks
	Ann Cosgrave	Elizabeth Cusack
	Emma Delahunty	Colette Doherty
	Ann Flood	Vivienne Gogarty
	Margaret Hawney	Niamh Hollingsworth
	Maura Kelly	Frieda Mc Donald
	Jean Mc Donnell	Hazel Mc Keon
	Rita Moran	Dolores Murphy
	Breda O'Shea	Frances Owens
	Jane Phelan	Kathleen Sweeney
	Aileen Telford	Sally Cranfield
	Olive Territt	
1967	Patricia Condron	Mary Connaughton
	Marie Connellan	Regina Corbett
	Cora Field	Elís Flanagan
	Marie Guilfoyle	Jean Horan
	Barbara Joyce	Marilyn Kerr
	Maritza Sinanan	Marie Walsh
	Catherine Whitaker	Patricia Campbell
	Geraldine Agnew	Mary McCrorry

YEAR	Students

1968

Avril Coleman	Sheelagh Crosbie
Nuala Dillon	Rita Doyle
Joan Dunleavy	Concepta Fahey
Maria Gallagher	Julienne Hession
Bernice Mahon	Gavaise Maher
Terry Moody	Fidelma Mundow
Rosemary McCallion	Clare McDonald
Kathleen Mc Nally	Catherine O'Brien
Gemma O'Connor	Dolores O'Farrell
Muriel Quinn	Mary Sheahan
Madeline Sweeney	Mary Grant

1969

Camilla Barry	Mary Bennett
Gwen Branigan	Paula Casey
Carmel Coakley	Monica Condron
Joan Crowley	Michelle Duane
Siobhan Dunleavy	Christine Gunne
Rhona Hegarty	Elaine Hughes
Emer Hynes	Geraldine Maguire
Pat Maher	Maureen Mooney
Maire Murphy	

1970

Jill Bannon	Eileen Barry
Ann Bird	Johanne Burke
Najet Charef	Una Connellan
Viola Crowley	Margaret Curley
Marie Doyle	Josephine Dunleavy
Mary Fegan	Mary Gavin
Ann Hession	Ann Humphries
Carol Hynes	Eithne McDermott
Mella Hynes	Monica Mc Gill
Deirdre Mc Manus	Maureen Mooney
Veronica O'Leary	Lindi Naughton

YEAR	**Students**	
1970	Marie Mooney	Cheryl Rawle
	Sheila Telford	Deirdre Pallard
	Pauline Rhatigan	Monica Whelan
	Marie Mooney	Carol Hynes
1971	Barbara Clery	Wendy de Freitas
	Ann Marie Flanagan	Clare Coleman
	Grainne Dillon	Hene Hardiman
	Gabriel Croke	Sandra Farrell
	Jean Igoe	Miriam Kelly
	Anna Magee	Mary Mc Hugh
	Rosemary Kelly	Jennifer Mullan
	Hilary Quinn	Virginia Kerr
	Gabriel Mc Callion	Nicola Quinsey
	Sheila Rodgers	Olivia Renehan
	Maureen Ruigrok	Susan Shannon
1972	Fiona Dixon	Lorna Dorman
	Florence Eivers	Ann Hoare
	Mary Hosty	Coleen Joyce
	Patricia Keane	Debbie Kelly
	Marion Minnock	Geraldine Mullen
	Ann Mac Mahon	Dee Mc Mahon
	Evelyn Mc Nabor	M. Elizabeth Nolan
	Noelle O'Donoghue	MaryAnn Sombunmntham
	Nora Stack	Hau Man Tam
	Ann Tyrrell	Siobhan Utley
	Siobhan Watson	Deirdre Byrne
	Gay Campion	Eithne Crotty
	Barbara Cluskey	Jacqueline Carney
	Sylvia Kelleher	

YEAR	Students	
1973	Sheila Kelty	Catherine Keane
	Phil. Mooney	Mary-Sue Moore
	Sandra Mullan	Noelle Murphy
	Sheila McCallion	Deirdre McGarry
	Bernie Nolan	Roisin O'Doherty
	Marie O'Gara	Debbie O'Connell
	Maureen Phelan	Rachel Rhatigan
	Indo Tanko	Fiona Watson
	S. Williams	Lynn Bissessan
	Mary Coffey	Mary Crowley
	Isolde Croke	Noelle Curley
	Judith Gavin	Claire Gibson
	Lopa Guha	June Hughes
	Margaret Hurley	Terry Pruden
1974	Clodagh Barry	Ann Bissessar
	Shelagh Carty	Adele Casey
	Deirdre Carmody	Patricia Casey
	Deirdre Carmody	Jean Daly
	M.A. Ferrari	Ely Ferris
	Nicola Gavin	Judy Gleeson
	Ger. Godfrey	Ad. Greene
	Ingrid Grysim	Marianne Franklin
	Susan Hill	Susan Horan
	Mary Igoe	Anna Kearns
	Mary Kinalan	Kath Merlehan
	Deirdre Moloney	Catherine Moore
	Alisa Mullan	Brenda Mulloy
	Margaret Nolan	Ann O'Byrne
	Mauread O'Connor	Phil O'Connor
	Margaret O'Doherty	Teresa O'Dwyer
	Marian O'Leary	Aideen O'Shea
	Phyllis O'Toole	Bernadette Quinn

YEAR	Students	
1974	Fiona Sheane	Geraldine Slevin
	Olive Taaffe	
1975	Betty Allen	Michelle Anderson
	Ruth Anderson	Mable Blake
	Anita Byrne	J. Cawley
	Maria Gavigan	Monica Gibson
	Ailish Hannon	Edel Hendron
	Mary Henry	Eilish Hewitt
	Betty Higgins	Sally Ann Kavanagh
	Eavan Kelly	Corene Lawless
	Sue Mayne	Niamh Mc Conn
	Claire Mc Entegert	Anne Mc Mullan
	Rosemary Mc Guinness	Anne O'Farrell
	Jocelyn Ormonde	Sandra Owens
	Consilia Parekh	Susan Phelan
	Pamela Ronan	Mercedes Slein
	Deirdre Slevin	
1976	Anise Bartosik	Bernadette Buckley
	Collette Byrne	Mary Byrne
	Cathy Casey	Ingrid Christenson
	Marion Clarke	Louise Donegan
	Eilish Farrell	Cecile Ferrare
	Mary Foster	Geraldine French
	Sheelagh Gaffney	Bernadette Gunne
	Rosemary Gunne	Brenda Hickey
	Hilary Howard	Esther Keaney
	Ann Marie Kearns	Mary Kelly
	Thérése Kennedy	Patricia Lord
	Eleanor Lorigan	Pamela Madigan
	Joan Mc Callion	Christina Mc Creevy
	Mary Mc Loughlin	Jessie Mc Lennion

YEAR	Students	
1976	Arabella O'Keeffe	Lan Ping Ng
	Elizabeth Quinsey	Rosemary Ronan
	Anna Ryan	Claire Ryan
	Ann Schaffeneker	Carol Taaffe
	Olivia Tam	Constance Whyte
	Michele Wright	
1977	Sara Ashe	Catriona Belton
	Marella Byrne	Phil Cantrell
	Miriam Carri	Anna Carrol
	Clodagh Conroy	Madeline Coleman
	Mary Downey	Dolores Egan
	Eileen Eivers	Deirdre Fitzpatrick
	Marguerite Gavigan	Anne Geoghegan
	Aoibheann Gibbons	Maria Gilsenan
	Jennifer Hill	Mary Houlihan
	Patricia Huston	Barbara Hurley
	Helen Kavanagh	Lorraine Kavanagh
	Ava Keenan	Celily Kelly
	Liz Kelly	Mary Kelly
	June Kiernan	Bernadette Leavy
	Aoife Leonard	Tina Lewis
	Berencia Macauley	Grainne McConn
	Etta Mc Keon	Gwen McEntaggart
	Christine McInerney	Anne McKillen
	Sharon Magee	Alison Marsh
	Paula Martin	Aileen Murphy
	Celine Nolan	Jean O'Connell
	Barbara O'Driscoll	Kathleen O'Mara
	Marie O'Reilly	Edel Porteus
	Antoinette Quinsey	Michelle Ridgeway
	Dorothy Ronan	Fiona Russell
	Tara Healy Singh	

YEAR	Students

1978		
	Adrienne Belton	Catriona Byrne
	Fiodhana Callanan	Siobhan Canty
	Obiogeli Chuckwoodimma	Charlotte Coyle
	Jean Culleton	Anne Cunningham
	Claire Dargan	Kathanne Kileen
	Helen Long	Avril Lyons
	Liz Mc Donald	Liz Mc Creevy
	Mora Mc Namara	Monica Mc Killeen
	Sarah Mc Guire	Mary Manning
	Ellen Marron	Anne Molloy
	Cathy Molloy	Rosemary Moriarity
	Mary Murphy	Caroline O'Connor
	Margaret O'Donnell	Mary O'Donohoe
	Jacqueline O'Driscoll	Audrey O'Sullivan
	Sinead Harte	Audrey Higgins
	Joan Higgins	Francis Kearns
	Paula Keegan	Jay Kelly
	Anne Kennedy	Sharon Kenedy
	Sarah Keogh	Marie Dillon
	Olga Dillon	Susan Donegan
	Rita Doran	Myra Doyle
	Anne Downey	Therese Dunne
	Veronica Francis	Sandra Gaher
	Dorenna Gavin	Janet Hanley
	Maeve Slein	Mary Sullivan
	Angela Tunney	Jane Ward
	Yvonne Whelan	Margaret Doddy
	Loreto Barrett	Janet Behan
	Sandra O'Sullivan	Grace O'Toole
	Sally O'Toole	Shelia Power
	Louise Gavin	Tina Rangel
	Fiona Reade	Linda Rickard
	Eileen Ridgeway	Louise Robinson
	Nessa Shevlin	

YEAR	Students

1979	Liz Alexander	Barbara Andreucetti
	Jackie Allan	Patricia Bale
	Susan Barrett	Mary Belton
	Marcella Blake	Ann Bruton
	Jackie Burke	Bar. Buggy
	Susan Coghlan	Deirdre Coleman
	Terry Connolly	Sonja Croke
	Clare Dargan	Yvonne Dillon
	Roseanne Donegan	Marie Donoghue
	Mary Doyle	Adreinne Dunne
	Aedeena Eiffe	Ruth Farrell
	Elizabeth Foster	Maise Gibbon
	Ann Hannigan	Jenny Haresych
	Lorretta Henelly	Bernice Hurley
	Jane Kavanagh	Ann Marie Kelly
	Hilda Kelly	Caroline Kiernan
	Greta King	Karen Lord
	Mary Lubbe	Maureen Mc Cabe
	Eileen Mc Callion	Catherine Mc Keon
	Christine Mc Cormack	Mary Moore
	Edwina Mullan	Anna Nolan
	Siobhan O'Brien	Jeanette O'Donnell
	Joan O'Donnell	Sandra O'Gorman
	Maeve O'Reilly	Jackie O'Shea
	Geraldine Power	Martine Quinn
	Patricia Ring	Patricia Roberts
	Linda Sheridan	Emer Slein
	Susan Stairs	Martina Verhulst
	Joan White	

1980	Aisling Carolan	Laura Clarke
	Barbara Cruise	Carol Cunningham
	Ann Maria Dargan	Margaret Delaney
	Jane Diffley	Sylvia Dillon

YEAR	Students

1980	Martine Dunne	Christine Flynn
	Dolores Foster	Suzanne Gaynor
	Carol Geraghty	Eileen Gibbons
	Eithne Gilespie	Emily Godson
	Nuala Hamilton	Joyce Hanratty
	Orla Harte	Colette Haughton
	Mary Higgins	Georgina Hoey
	Alva Hope-Ross	Azelie Houlihan
	Linda Kavanagh	Lucy Keane
	Rachel Keogh	Claire Kinnane
	Orla Lehane	Lorraine Lewis
	Charlotte Lubbe	Rose-Ann Lynch
	Therese Macken	Eilish Martin
	Colette McAuliffe	Yvonne Mc Cabe
	Fiona Mc Conn	Anne-Marie McConnell
	Catherine Mc Donald	Sarah Mc Gann
	Brenda Mc Elligott	Fiona Mc Govern
	Karen Mc Hugh	Siobhan Mc Inerney
	Marion Mc Keone	Julie Moore
	Mary Moran	Anne-Marie Murphy
	Sheila Murphy	Rita Nolan
	Patricia Ogbuli	Aisling O'Connell
	Elaine O'Connor	Lilian O'Driscoll
	Susan O'Gorman	Frances O'Neill
	Rosemary O'Sullivan	Amanda Phelan
	Catherine Ring	Mary Shaw
	Orla Sheridan	Margaret Sherry
	Maeve Shevlin	Rena Smith
	Catherine Stafford	Hilary Tonge
	Serena Belton	Liz Blake
	Pauline Brennan	Anne-Marie Broderick
	Miriam Buggy	Margaret Cantrell

YEAR	Students

1981		
	Patsy Bodkin	Julie Bury
	Olive Byrne	Ann Marie Callanan
	Celine Carey	Marina Cassidy
	Shelagh Coghlan	Caroline Condron
	Paula Culleton	Pauline Darragh
	Ciara Dillon	Patricia Donegan
	Marie Dooley	Geraldine Doyle
	Anne Dunne	Bernadette Dunne
	Catherine Finlay	Grainne Flanagan
	Caroline Fullam	Catherine Giovanelli
	Corena Glennon	Mairéad Glennon
	Suzi Godson	Catherine Gorey
	Patricia Gormley	Karen Gormley
	Natalie Haccius	Deirdre Hannigan
	Edel Hurley	Jackie Kavanagh
	Liz Keaney	Paula Kearns
	Charmaine Keenan	Michelle Keenan
	Judy Kelly	Marguerite Kenny
	Paula Lawlor	Anna Logan
	Mary Lynam	Catherine McCreevy
	Hilda Mc Laughlin	Detta Macken
	Patricia Manning	Carol Millington
	Janet Moloney	Caroline Mooney
	Leonie Murphy	Claire O'Connell
	Emer O'Keeffe	Geraldine O'Kelly
	Róisín O'Ceallaigh	Oonagh O'Leary
	Gillian O'Loughlin	Emma O'Sullivan
	Angela Penny	Marie Penny
	Maureen Power	Louise Prendergast
	Erin Rajah	Fiona Rajah
	Audrey Robinson	Lorraine Shanahan
	Sally Sudbury	Tina Sheedy
	Ann Tuite	

YEAR	**Students**	
1982	Eleanor Barrett	Mary Barrett
	Dolores Boden	Deirdre Bodkin
	Lucy Borthwick	Bernadette Brady
	Dorothy Brady	Geraldine Brennan
	Mary Brennan	Deborah Burke
	Bridgina Burke	Geraldine Byrne
	Frances Byrne	Miriam Conway
	Jean Cummins	Siobhan Cunningham
	Nuala Darragh	Colette Dillon
	Jackie Doddy	Aisling Drury
	Caroline Dunne	Joan Finlay
	Maria Dunne	Siobhan Flynn
	Catherine Foster	Fionuala Giblin
	Ornat Hartigan	Ann Ivors
	Gwen Kavanagh	Rosemary Kenny
	Siobhan Larkin	Karen Lee
	Carol Little	Valja Mc Cabe
	Carmel Mc Cormack	Ann Mc Donald
	Maeve Mc Elligott	Louise Mc Guinness
	Anna Marie Mc Inerney	Nola McLaughlin
	Maria Mc Morrow	Lorna Mc Grory
	Rosena Mc Shane	Marisa Maguire
	Caroline Malone	Maura Marron
	Catherine Milner	Linda Molloy
	Orla Murphy	Sandra Murphy
	Niamh Mulryan	Ursula Noctor
	Lisa Nolan	Geraldine O'Callaghan
	Karen O'Donnell	Niamh O'Donnell
	Orla O'Donohoe	Mairéad O'Riordain
	Jackie Penrose	Finnula Peters
	Helen Reid	Elizabeth Richardson
	Fiona Roantree	Maria Scallon
	Olive Walshe	Lorraine Whelan
	Iseult White	Sr. Rowena

YEAR	Students	
1983	Antoinette Assaf	Emer Bagnall
	Dora Banks	Noreen Barrett
	Una Bolger	Helen Brannigan
	Ann Brennan	Finola Bruton
	Grace Bruton	Mary Cassells
	Geraldine Caulfield	Catherine Convery
	Avril Corcoran	Catherine Crehan
	Ashling Culleton	Lucy Danaher
	Deirdre D'arcy	Helen Doherty
	Patricia Dardis	Deborah Donnelly
	Sharon Donohoe	Geraldine Donovan
	Marisa Drury	Brenda Dunne
	Siobhan Dunne	Teresa Dunne
	Susan Dowdall	Jean Errity
	Irene Farrell	Niamh Farrell
	Deirdre Fenton	Deirdre Fitzpatrick
	Martine Fitzpatrick	Siobhan Fullam
	Fiona Ginnell	Brona Goulding
	Sonja Haccius	Mary Hands
	Clodagh Kavanagh	Ann Kelly
	Catherine Kelly	Shivaun Kelly
	Finola King	Sharon Lawlor
	Louisa Lenihan	Mairead Little
	Sophia Lubbe	Cecilia Lynch
	Rosemary Maffen	Teresa Magee
	Helen Maguire	Celeste Martins
	Mary Molloy	Bernadette Moriarty
	Kathryn Murray	Katrina Mc Cormack
	Clare Mc Govern	Mary Mc Shane
	Maeve Naughton	Adobi Nwokedi
	Dorothy O'Byrne	Sandra O'Gorman
	Janice O'Neill	Gráinne O'Reilly
	Jacqueline O'Sullivan	Lucy O'Sullivan
	Ann Prendergast	Aideen Prendergast

YEAR	Students

1983	Aideen Quigley	Edel Quinn
	Sinead Redmond	Áine Scallon
	Matilda Sheeran	Jackie Smith
	Helen Stack	Mary Sylver
	Nicola Wall	Niamh Whyte
	Emma Williams	

1984	Claudia Basini	Anne M. Baxter
	Denise Bernie	Aideen Bodkin
	Orla Branagan	Áine Briody
	Audrey Browne	Margaret Buggy
	Emma Byrne	Nicola Cahill
	Siobhan Carnegie	Fiona Casey
	Suzanne Casey	Geraldine Cassells
	Clare Conway	Paula Corcoran
	Anne Curran	Lisa Donohoe
	Rachel Doyle	Siobhan Duffy
	Antonia Fennell	Maria Fitzharris
	Pauline Fitzpatrick	Martha Frances
	Oonagh Geoghegan	Maria Gleeson
	Mairead Higgins	Siobhan Hammond
	Adrienne Henshaw	Sharon Kearney
	Clodagh Keegan	Allyson Kelly
	Ann Kelly	Geraldine Kelly
	Fiona Lawlor	Stephanie Larkin
	Fiona Leahy	Joan Martin
	Brigid Mc Cabe	Anne M. Mc Cague
	Jean Mc Shane	Rachel Martin
	Janice Millington	Karen Monaghan
	Natasha Moore	Paula Morrin
	Michelle Mullally	Ann Mulvin
	Grace Murray	Fiona Murray
	Maria Murphy	Jennifer O'Connell
	Gráinne O'Connor	Deirdre O'Kelly

YEAR	Students	
1984	Miriam O'Kelly	Adrienne O'Neill
	Clodagh O'Reilly	Sharon O'Sullivan
	Roshene Pickering	Edel Prunty
	Helen Quigley	Mary Reilly
	Angela Rickard	Niamh Roantree
	Ann Marie Robinson	Orla Sheedy
	Colette Sylver	Orla Teahan
	Ciara Thornberry	Margaret Toolan
	Siobhan Tuite	Orla Tunney
	Emma Walsh	
1985	Jane Anderson	Paula Andreucetti
	Stephania Bassini	Maria Bourke
	Noeleen Carolan	Audrey Clince
	Tatiana Convery	Audrey Cowzer
	Deirdre Cronolly	Jacqueline Crowley
	Tracey Cullen	Edel Culleton
	Aideen Dolan	Suzanne Donovan
	Denise Doran	Valerie Downes
	Lisa Doyle	Nuala Doyle
	Brenda Fahey	Ann Paula Finnegan
	Susan Fenton	Deirdre Fitzgerald
	Deirdre Fogarty	Eimear Fogarty
	Ann Gleeson	Siobhán Gormley
	Caroline Harte	Mary Higgins
	Siobhan Hyde	Aveen Kehoe
	Cliona Kelliher	Brenda Kidd
	Barbara Kierans	Aileen Kilfeather
	Niamh Kinnane	Lavinia Kirwan
	Daire Laffin	Maria Leydon
	Fiona Lyons	Gillian Lyons
	Anne-Marie Mc Gauran	Caroline Menton
	Helen Molloy	Rose Molloy
	Kathleen Mulally	Patricia Mulvin

YEAR	Students	
1985	Lorraine Murphy	Elaine Murray
	Siobhán Noctor	Frances Odlum
	Susan O'Donoghue	Barbara O'Neill
	Lorna O'Rahilly	Andrea Penrose
	Darina Phelan	Anne-Marie Quigley
	Fiona Reilly	Lisa Rogers
	Helen Sexton	Siobhán Sheehan
	Leenane Shiels	Yvonne Sheridan
	Lorraine Smith	Lorraine Sweeney
	Katie Walsh	Eileen Wall
1986	Ruth Armstrong	Jacqueline Barker
	Mary Begley	Carol Bohan
	Michaela Boylan	Geraldine Brady
	Michelle Brady	Roisin Brannigan
	Mary Brazil	Marguerite Burke
	Mary Burke	Susannah Carr
	Suzanne Caulfield	Carina Claffey
	Anne-Marie Connellan	Aideen Cooney
	Debbie Conroy	Brenda Corcoran
	Ruth Corcoran	Margaret Courtney
	Sharon Cronin	Jennifer Crookes
	Eileen Cullen	Rhona D'arcy
	Sharon Daly	Sheila Diffley
	Jane Donegan	Rachelle Donohoe
	Janet Donnelly	Samantha Downing
	Anne Marie Doyle	Caroline Doyle
	Ailish Doyle	Celine Dunne
	Sylvia Egan	Sarah Farrell
	Anne-Marie Finnegan	Olwyn Fitzpatrick
	Rita Fitzpatrick	Serena Fogarty
	Niamh Foran	Nicola Gogan
	Marie-Louise Goodwin	Hilary Gormley
	Gillian Grant	Elizabeth Hammond

YEAR	Students	
1986	Niamh Holmes	Lesley Jones
	Gina Kavanagh	Joan Keaney
	Mary Kelly	Mary-Paula Kelly
	Janet Keogh	Siobhan Killeen
	Susan Killoran	Deirdre Leahy
	Jean Leahy	Emer Leogue
	Anita Lynch	Ruth Martin
	Jane Martin	Geraldine Mc Cabe
	Margaret Mc Cabe	Marie Mc Crea
	Sinead Mc Cormack	Vera Mc Govern
	Debbie Mc Glone	Deirdre Mc Elliott
	Fiona Mc Intyre	Mary Jo Morrin
	Fiona Murphy	Suzanne Monaghan
	Adrienne Nolan	Niamh O'Brien
	Mary O'Connor	Emer O'Donnell
	Irene O'Gorman	Olwyn O'Malley
	Emer O'Neill	Sheera O'Sullivan
	Claire Scallon	Rachel Sherry
	Kirsty Shiels	Michelle Tobin
	Lisa Toland	Anna Williams
	Anne-Marie Willetts	Siobhan Wogan
1987	Emma Barnes	Jon. Barrett
	Niamh Barry	Melanie Baxter
	Inez Bernie	Sharon Bodkin
	Katherine Bourke	Caroline Brady
	Joan Brennan	Julie Byrne
	Therese Byrne	Sally A. Cafferty
	Sharon Cahill	Linda Churchward
	Carol Clancy	Liz Collins
	Carmel Condon	Carol Cooke
	Fiona Corbet	Carol Courtney
	Edel Cunningham	Tara Daly
	Natalie Dinsmore	Alice Donnelly

YEAR	Students

1987

Rhona Doris — Edel Duffy
Kayona Fagan — Caroline Farrell
Grainne Flynn — Aoife Gibney
Geraldine Gleeson — Suzanne Goodwin
Emma Greene — Catherine Hallahan
Aisling Hammond — Michelle Hannon
Anita Harrison — Sarah Higgins
Betina Jordan — Denise Kelly
Ruth Kelly — Doreen Kilfeather
Aideen King — Thérèse Leonard
Emer Little — Emma Loomes
Louise Lynn — Niamh Madigan
Elsa Martins — Louise Mc Govern
Margaret Mc Grane — Margaret Mc Kernan
Patricia Mc Namara — Anne Marie Melody
Audrey Mulcahy — Lynda Mullan
Amanda Murray — Jill Nolan
Kerri Nolan — Natalie Nuytten
Clodagh O'Donovan — Caitriona O'Grady
Tara O'Kelly — Sinead O'Leary
Justine O'Reilly — Helena Quane
Joanne Quigley — Annette Quinn
Miriam Regan — Gillian Ridgeway
Anne Ryan — Catherine Sexton
Michelle Smith — Helen Stairs
Louise Tolan — Ann Marie Walsh

1988

Kirsten Asaa — Orla Boggan
Rochella Boggan — Lisa Brady
Michelle Brady — Cliona Brennan
Natasha Byram — Kira Byrne
Eilish Carnegie — Nicola Canavan
Elaine Cockram — Eunice Cogan
Lorraine Corcoran — Audrey Cullen

149

YEAR	Students

1988

Elizabeth Cullen	Celine Davis
Sarah Dowling	Siobhan Dunne
Debbie Dwyer	Jennifer Egan
Hilary Eustace	Eileen Fallon
Orla Fallon	Charlotte Fennell
Louise Gaffney	Sharon Gallagher
Catherine Gleeson	Shauna Greely
Laura Hallahan	Ciara Halligan
Sonia Hannon	Valerie Healy
Ruth Henshaw	Barbara Kavanagh
Sarah Kelly	Sonia Killoran
Clodagh Lanigan	Cara Larkin
Jane Lubbe	Gail Lynch
Susan Lynch	Liz Lyons
Finula Maguire	Mairead Mahon
Bronagh Mallaghan	Bridin Mannion
Ruth Mannion	Gillian Matthews
Michelle Maxwell	Patricia Mc Cabe
Audrey Mc Cann	Hazel Mc Carthy
Ciara Mc Cormack	Carol Mc Donnell
Barbara Mc Gauran	Vivienne Mc Keon
Karen Mc Laughlin	Tracy Millington
Lorna Molloy	Susan Molloy
Niamh Mullahy	Carol Mullins
Klara Munnelly	Vivien Murphy
Cliona Murray	Grainne Murray
Sinead O'Brien	Liz O'Connor
Osna O'Connor	Sinead O'Donohoe
Carol O'Sullivan	Jacqueline O'Sullivan
Sinead Penrose	Lorna Pentz
Debra Reilly	Erika Reilly
Emma Rickard	Nora Roberts
Elaine Ryan	Maria Sheeran
Yvonne Sweeney	Margie Tuthill

150

YEAR	Students	
1988	Ann Marie Tyrrell	Suzanne Walsh
1989	Mary Behan	Aisling Boggan
	Fiona Bolger	Karen Boyle
	Suzanne Brady	Martha Brennan
	Niamh Byrne	Niamh Canavan
	Fiona Carolan	Orla Carolan
	Gillian Clarke	Fiona Clince
	Mary Collins	Aisling Connolly
	Lisa Connolly	Mary Lou D'arcy
	Deirdre Dalton	Dara Devlin
	Margaret Diamond	Jennifer Donovan
	Grace Doyle	Jennifer Egan
	Keelin Egan	Aideen Eyres
	Nicola Finnegan	Ciara Gibney
	Ferga Gleeson	Maeve Gleeson
	Gemma Grant	Rachel Greene
	Sheena Groome	Elaine Hayes
	Mary Keaney	Catriona Keating
	Clare Kelly	Tina Kelly
	Hillary Kennedy	Julianne Kirwan
	Olive Leddy	Sorcha Leydon
	Petrina Loughran	Orflaith Lynch
	Clare Madigan	Edel Martin
	Audrey Maxwell	Sandra McCaghy
	Rachel McDonald	Mary McEntire
	Sarah Mc Nicholas	Suzanne Meleady
	Lisa Melody	Fiona Monaghan
	Ann Marie Moran	Susan Moriarty
	Louise Mullan	Ciara Murphy
	Erin Murphy	Louise Nelson
	Justine O'Brien	Mary O'Brien
	Sheila O'Brien	Susan O'Brien
	Patricia O'Donnell	Maria O'Donohoe

YEAR	Students	
1989	Patricia O'Farrell	Susan O'Gorman
	Ann Marie O'Keeffe	Martha O'Neill
	Sarah O'Neill	Samantha O'Reilly
	Michelle Pemberton	Maria Phelan
	Niamh Proudfoot	Tanya Quinn
	Miriam Reid	Judy Rudden
	Fidelma Ryan	Laura Sexton
	Colette Shanahan	Lisa Sheeran
	Astrid Smith	Barbara Staines
	Ruth Stanley	Ciara Swan
	Karen Touhey	Orla Tyrrell
	Sinead Vaughan	Ciara Walshe
	Louise Walshe	Kathleen Wymes
	Grainne Young	Siobhan Young
1990	Catherine Bourke	Michelle Boylan
	Sinead Brady	Katherine Brennan
	Valerie Brophy	Grainne Brosnan
	Jennifer Browne	Patricia Burns
	Sharon Butterly	Amanda Byran
	Catherine Byrne	Aywleen Carroll
	Ciara Clune	Deirdre Coleman
	Fionnuala Conway	Ciara Crookes
	Shona Culhane	Aisling Delaney
	Eimear Gleeson	Niamh Greely
	Aoife Griffith	Edwina Garland
	Helen Gilsenan	Judith Giltinane
	Linda Feightrey	Donna Finan
	Susan Flavin	Evelyn Eyres
	Sinead Fallon	Olwyn Farrell
	Joanne Doyle	Mary Doyle
	Sinead Doyle	Emma Delaney
	Eleanor Doody	Orla Dowling
	Edel Lennon	Beth Lennox

YEAR	Students	
1990	Jennifer Lynch	Selena Kenny
	Criona Laffan	Anne Marie Leahy
	Jennifer Jackson	Honor Kavanagh
	Gillian Kelly	Anne Marie Flynn
	Sheena Hickey	Karen Hogan
	Karen Lynch	Una Magner
	Denise Mahon	Deborah Mallaghan
	Yvonne Meredith	Julie Mc Carthy
	Eimear Mc Mahon	Orla Mc Namara
	Ciara Mc Quillan	Orla Mitton
	Wendy Monks	Sarah Jane Mooney
	Yvonne Ankers	Carol Barron
	Edel Boles	Lesley Moran
	Orla Murphy	Mary Murtagh
	Gillian Musgrave	Anne Marie Purcell
	Geraldine Quinn	Niamh Leogue
	Deborah Loughran	Phillipa Wall
	Judith Walsh	Ruth Wogan
	Samantha Smith	Eimear Teahan
	Heidi Vambeck	Emily Richardson
	Ann Marie Ryan	Sheila Ryan
1991	Alison Brady	Louise Brannagan
	Sarah Brennan	Claudine Byrne
	Pamela Byrne	Sandra Byrne
	Ann Marie Cleary	Ruth Connolly
	Realtin Cronin	Suzanne Cronin
	Carmel Cullen	Anne D'Arcy
	Audrey D'Arch	Justine Delaney
	Karen Donohue	Sinead Dowling
	Anne Mary Dunne	Deirdre Fahy
	Eva Fallon	Rosemary Dunne
	Petrina Farrell	Elaine Flanagan
	Heidi Flanagan	Erika Fox

YEAR	Students	
1991	Paula Gilmartin	Deirdre Glennon
	Claire Griffin	Roisin Harrison
	Tara Hegarty	Caoimhe Henderson
	Sharon Kavanagh	Patricia Keary
	Liza Kelly	Phillipa Kenny
	Susan Kenny	Jane Killoran
	Fiona Larkin	Sinead Leahy
	Christine Linehan	Niamh Loughran
	Caoimhe Lynch	Tara Lynch
	Niamh Lyons	Paula Mc Cabe
	Jane Mc Carthy	Mary Mc Carthy
	Louise Mc Gauran	Therese Mc Keone
	Deborah Mc Loughlinn	Margaret Mc Myler
	Nicola Mooney	Ann Moriarty
	Sandra Murphy	Jennifer Nelson
	Dympna Nolan	Lisa Nolan
	Gillian O'Brien	Michelle O'Brien
	Tara O'Connor	Clare O'Donnell
	Orlagh O'Dowd	Andrea O'Loughlin
	Sarah O'Meara	Yvonne O'Neill
	Mary O'Rourke	Kelly O'Sullivan
	Olga Owens	Phillipa Pentz
	Fiona Quane	Aoife Rickard
	Barbara Ridgway	Ciara Rooney
	Joanne Ryan	Elizabeth Sherwin
	Sarah Jane St. Ledger	Karen Sweeney
	Jane Taaffe	Carolyn Tierney
	Samantha Tierney	Sonia Varadkar
	Audrey Ward	Aoife Whelan
	Avril Yeates	Cara Mc Loughlin
1992	Aoife Brennan	Susan Bradley
	Deirdre Behan	Sinead Caffrey
	Martina Byrne	Nicola Butterly

YEAR	Students	
1992	Orla Cooney	Noreen Corr
	Sheila Brennan	Lynda Brocklebank
	Crona Briody	Nichol Connolly
	Jennifer Churchward	Philippa Casey
	Deirdre Carroll	Orla Canavan
	Yvette Dunne	Nessa Curran
	Lisa Cullen	Niamh Crookes
	Corona Cosgrave	Niamh Browne
	Rhona Brennan	Maria Corbet
	Clodagh Gunnigle	Cliona Flanagan
	Aoife Egan	Alison Kindlon
	Aine Killeen	Niamh Keating
	Alison Musgrave	Claire Murray
	Dympna Harmey	Chantal Hourihan
	Ruth Kavanagh	Samantha Kirwan
	Orla Mc Intyre	Louise Mc Cormack
	Eleanor Molloy	Rosemary Martin
	Aisling Lynch	Elisa Nardone
	Blathnaid Mc Cormack	Mary Mc Namara
	Elaine Lovett	Babita Jain
	Jean Harmon	Margaret Mc Cauley
	Olga Nolan	Aoife Nolan
	Niamh O'Neill	Carla O'Neill
	Stella O'Malley	Catherine O'Brien
	Aoife O'Beirne	Leigh Ryan
	Creena Ryan	Aisling Ryan
	Deirdre O'Dowd	Mary O'Donnell
	Dianne Nelson	Niamh O'Sullivan
	Mairead Reynolds	Cronagh Ryan
	Karen Watters	Cliona Wong
	Karen Wogan	Fiona Smith
	Elizabeth Reynolds	Eileen O'Sullivan
	Margarita Farrell	

YEAR	Students	
1993	Margaret Horan	Siu Lam
	Sorcha Whelan	Avril Bailey
	Ciara Bell	Anne Brady
	Catherine Brady	Sinead Brennan
	Elizabeth Brennan	Lorraine Bresnan
	Avril Brophy	Susan Browne
	Ann Marie Butler	Susan Campbell
	Claire Carter	Natasha Caulfield
	Joanne Christian	Emma Coakley
	Suzanne Cockram	Niamh Condron
	Helen Corcoran	Lisa Cowley
	Susan Cox	Tara Cawley
	Elizabeth Cronin	Nicola Cronin
	Gillian Culhane	Cliodhna Daly
	Geraldine Desmond	Emma Doyle
	Audrey De Lacy	Marie Eustace
	Dervala Farrell	Andrea Fassnidge
	Eimear Fitzgerald	Anne Fitzpatrick
	Treasa Gibney	Mary Giltinane
	Joanna Gray	Ann Marie Guiney
	Sarah Jane Gunne	Ailbhe Henderson
	Sarah Hodson	Vivienne Horkan
	Anita Hughes	Nicola Hyland
	Nicola Jackson	Patricia Jordan
	Emma Kearney	Margaret Keavney
	Ruth Kennedy	Anne Kennedy
	Edel King	Jennifer Kirby
	Lizanna Kirwan	Jennifer Kirwan
	Anne Marie Lawlor	Emma Linehan
	Fiona Loughran	Darelle Lynch
	Laura Lynch	Sarah Jane Mc Donnell
	Hilda Mc Keone	Evelyn Mulcahy
	Patricia Mulligan	Karen Murphy
	Lynn Murray	Susanne O'Brien

YEAR	Students

1993

Roisin O'Byrne	Sharon O'Gorman
Helen O'Neill	Jane Prendergast
Una Prunty	Janette Quinn
Niamh Robinson	Sinead Ryan
Lisa Shiels	Jane Skelly
Adele Spiller	Olivia Swayne
Clare Taaffe	Deirdre Threadgold
Catherine Toole	Alma Tyrrell
Caroline Walsh	Sinead Walshe
Sorcha O'Flanagan	

1994

Emma Branagan	Anna Carthy
Jane Terry	Samantha Smith
Eimear Bell	Audrey Bermingham
Yvonne Boylan	
Kathleen Donoghue	Saoirse Doyle
Jennifer Garvey	Tania Gaynor
Caroline Hansberry	Sinead O'Neill
Shannon Lyon	Emma Tighe
Deirdre Maye	Jennifer Kinirons
Eimear Mc Ginn	Lorraine Mc Nerney
Eileen Mooney	Oonagh O'Brien
Gillian O'Byrne	Teresa O'Donnell
Karen Corbet	Lorraine Allis
Sinead Delaney	Alison Fagan
Elaine Fassnidge	Karen Connolly
Grace Cosgrove	Karen Cosgrove
Sarah Jane Fitzpatrick	Barbara Fogarty
Karen Henry	Eimear Hickey
Alma Jordan	Cora Lennon
Elizabeth Loughnane	Niamh Mc Cormack
Leon Mc Namara	Sarah Mongey
Naoimi O'Connor	Orla O'Sullivan
Nicola Patten	Gillian Quinlan

YEAR	Students	
1994	Tanya Sweeney	Fiona Brown
	Temitope Adegbola	Yvonne Bailey
	Sheena Barrett	Aoife Brennan
	Jennifer Canavan	Nina Caryol
	Donna Boyle	Isabel Claffey
	Maria Dinsmore	Jill Drennan
	Emma Fahey	Edelle Flynn
	Corine Hickey	Catherine Kehoe
	Lindsay Mc Cormack	Hazel Mc Greal
	Gemma Mooney	Caroline Murphy
	Claire O'Gorman	Dara Ruane
	Fiona Sheridan	Clara Smith
	Sinead Whelan	Ursula Clarke
	Aoife Clune	Sinead Clarke
	Regina De Burca	Aine Dunleavy
	Maria Fitzgerald	Catherine Guilfoyle
	Niamh Hurley	Ruth Kavanagh
	Victoria Keating	Marian Little
	Linda Lovett	Therese Mc Allister
	Aine Mc Cabe	Carol Mc Gowan
	Susan Moran	Rachel Murray
	Una O'Connor	Niamh O'Connor
	Orla O'Connor	Eilish O'Reilly
	Ann Marie Proudfoot	Fiona Rafter
	Caroline Reynolds	Eimear Brennan
	Jane Casey	Ruth Casey
	Sinead Cogan	Bree Cullen
	Emma Farrelly	Aine Fox
	Clodagh Groome	Jennifer Hussey
	Ann Marie Hyland	Aifric Hyland
	Catherine Kelly	Eileen Maguire
	Barbara Mahon	Helen Mc Loughlinn
	Louise Mc Nally	Nicola Meyler
	Bevin Power Mooney	Charlotte Morgan

YEAR	Students	
1994	Emma Moriarty	Laura Mulcahy
	Dearbhla Nic Nioclais	Katherine O'Callaghan
	Jennifer Quinn	
1995	Orla Walsh	Ciara Brady
	Jennifer Campbell	Celsus Cullen
	Ciara Drennan	Cathy Ennis
	Laura Fitzgerald	Angie Gallagher
	Sinead Ganly	Jennifer Grimes
	Anne Marie Hynes	Aoife Loughnane
	Carla Maguire	Paula Mc Shane
	Sarah Mc Carthy	Rachel Sweeney
	Antoinette Murphy	Susan Musgrave
	Karen Nolan	Sandra O'Gorman
	Mary O'Shea	Elizabeth Bourke
	Siobhan Carroll	Ellen Connis
	Karen Corbet	Denise Doyle
	Niamh Flinter	Fiona Gibbs
	Catherine Hegarty	Fiona Lynch
	Elaine Maher	Elaine Mc Caughley
	Clodagh Mc Donagh	Abigail Mc Mahon
	Edel O'Brien	Aoife O'Connor
	Suzanne O'Loughlin	Elisa Pirolla
	Lisa Porter	Christine Rafter
	Jean Roden	Deirdre Slyne
	Catherine Vallely	Margaret Walsh
	Catherine Walsh	Aoife Daly
	Catherine Bermingham	Cliona Boyle
	Kyrsta Brady	Aisling Brennan
	Janice Barker	Wendy Byrne
	Caitriona Conway	Emma Culhane
	Karen Cullen	Noelle Fox
	Amanda Gray	Niamh Brady

YEAR	**Students**	
1995	Orla Brosnan	Elizabeth Butterly
	Deirdre Costello	Lauren Delaney
	Niamh Donovan	Elizabeth Fay
	Ailbhe Gaffney	Eimear Greely
	Barbara Griffin	Nicola Hosie
	Helen Kampff	Alison Martin
	Sinead Moran	Hilary Murray
	Geraldine O'Hagan	Pamela Reid
	Julie Ann Somers	Elizabeth Tolan
	Niamh Trears	Vanessa Wilson
	Rhonda Reihill	Donna Ward
	Sinead Harmey	Siobhan Kearney
	Lorna Kennedy	Anne Marie Kilfeather
	Evonne Mann	Sarah Mc Nerney
	Emily Morgan	Kelly O'Halloran
	Sarah O'Leary	Nicola O'Neill
	Fidelma O'Sullivan	Pat Power Mooney
1996	Caitriona Allis	Alison Bell
	Caoimhe Boylan	Louise Boylan
	Lorna Brennan	Kathryn Burns
	Sarah Jane Byrne	Kerrie Byrne
	Ciara Cahill	Aoife Callaghan
	Susan Carroll	Niamh Carty
	Helena Corbett	Suzanne Coughlan
	Victoria Cullen	Caroline Cunningham
	Ada Delaney	Aoife Donohoe
	Sarah Doody	Linda Farragher
	Gwendoline Farrelly	Emma Flanagan
	Tara Fleming	Claire Hague
	Maura Healy	Avril Kavanagh
	Lisa Kenny	Ciara Mc Carthy
	Maria Mc Carthy	Niamh Mc Ginn
	Karen Mc Loughlin	Catherine Miller

YEAR	Students

1996

Audrey Mitton	Regina Mohan
Gemma Monaghan	Lidia Nardone
Michelle Nolan	Aoife O'Brien
Aideen O'Brien	Sinead O'Connor
Maria O'Dowd	Aoife O'Farrell
Davina Ody	Rachel Phelan
Danielle Power	Caroline Sheehan
Keelin Terry	Eimear Threadgold
Gillian Wall	Aine Whelan

1997

Asaa, Liesl	Bolton, Jillian
Boylan, Aifric Mary	Brocklebank, Laura
Butler, Lisa	Carpenter, Ailbhe
Carroll, Nicola	Casey, Hannah
Conroy, Jennifer	Cowley, Elaine
Cunningham, Cara	Curley, Deirdre
Darwish, Sonia	Delaney, Caoimhe
Doherty, Karen	Edwards, Clodagh
Fahy, Frances	Fenton, Sarah
Flanagan, Dearbhla	Gunn, Emma Louise
Hall, Irene	Hannan, Stacey
Harris, Gwendolyn	Heffernan, Maria
Henshaw, Maria	Hill, Yvonne
Hobbs, Iarla	Hogan, Aoife
Holmes, Emma Jane	Hyland, Emma-Jane
Ibanez Llongueras, Miriam	Kavanagh, Lorna Jane
Kenny, Una Marie	Lennon, Aedamar
Lennon, Lisa	Lynch, Claire
Mahon, Sarah Kathleen	McEntee, Bronwyn
McGoldrick, Barbara	McGourty, Samera
McLernon, Lucy	Memery, Linda
Molloy, Deirdre Mary	Mullaney, Lisa Ann
O'Dea, Sinead	Phelan, Anna

YEAR	Students
1997	Pickett, Maria Porter, Sabrina

YEAR   Students

1997

Pickett, Maria — Porter, Sabrina
Quinn, Geraldine — Rafter, Mary
Rickard, Eilish — Salmon, Aoife
Sheehan, Alison — Slamon, Fiona
Thompson, Emma — Tierney, Keelin
Toner, Sonya — Traynor, Georgina
Tyrrell, Grainne — Whelan, Grainne

1998

Ackerley, Anne-Marie — Aherne, Ciara Mary
Argue, Ciara — Billings, Aideen
Bolger, Michelle — Boylan, Amy Vivienne
Boylan, Maeve — Browne, Vivienne
Byrne, Sarah — Cahill, Anita Mary
Campbell, Fiona — Carty, Sharon Jane
Casey, Márie Bríd — Christian, Gemma
Cockram, Caroline — Collins, Jessica
Connon, Ailbhe — Conway, Melissa
Cooney, Rosemarie — Cousins, Kelley-Ann
Cunningham, Orlagh — Curran, Treasa Marie
Dalton, Niamh — Darmody, Claire
Donohoe, Nicola — Duffy, Corinna
Dunning, Andrea — Flanagan, Aoife
Flanagan, Jennifer — Gaynor, Rebecca
Glennon, Pauline — Gogic, Nadja
Good, Sarah — Granville, Marina
Gunn, Rebecca — Hanley, Claire
Hanley, Jessica — Harte, Deirdre
Healy, Marguerite — Henderson, Fiona
Hogan, Niamh — Hosie, Karen
Houlihan, Lorna — Kearney, Rebecca
Kelly, Louise — Kelly, Marie Therese
Kelly, Roisin — Killeen, Stephanie
Kirwan, Caroline — Lawlor, Rebecca
Lynch, Helen — McCarthy, Anita

YEAR	Students

1998

McCauley, Geraldine	McCormack, Muireann
McEvoy, Mandy	McGoldrick, Danielle
McHenry, Orla	McHugh, Louise
McLoughlin, Catherine	McNamara, Aoife
McNiffe, Deirdre	McVeigh, Eimear
Miller, Claire-Elaine	Mooney, Mairead
Mooney, Susan	Musgrave, Louise
Nelson, Gillian	Nolan, Heather
Ní Chuinneag·in, Aislinn	O'Brien, Claire
O'Brien, Orla	O'Connor, Sinead
O'Loughlin, Rebecca	O'Reilly, Marcella
O'Reilly, Siobhan	O'Riordan, Valerie
O'Sullivan, Ashling	O'Toole, Margaret
Pocock, Carolyn	Prenderville, Ruth
Puri, Manmeet Kaur	Reid, Joanne
Rice, Lorraine	Scrivener, Sinead
Slamon, Maeve	Spollen, Sinead
Sweetnam, Adrienne	Treacy, Karen
Veale, Emma	Walsh, Gillian
Walsh, Sarah	de Lacy, Helen Louise

1999

Barrett, Rachel	Barron, Lynn
Bradley, Louise	Brannigan, Rebecca
Brennan, Blaithin	Briody, Niamh
Byrne, Claire	Carroll, Rachel
Carthy, Elaine	Christian, Alison
Clince, Annette	Conway, Yvonne
Corbet, Nicola	Corcoran, Sarah
Costello, Niamh	Cronin, Barbara
Cusack, Caitriona	Delaney, Marie
Demetriou, Lara	Dixon, Deirdre
Dorney, Laura	Downes, Catherine
Drennan, Denise	Farragher, Maria
Fenton, Angie	Finnegan, Louise

163

YEAR	Students	
1998	Flanagan, Lynn	Flynn, Laura
	Gallagher, Aoife	Ganly, Ciara
	Garland, Marianne	Gear, Maeve
	Gilhawley, Deirdre	Gilson, Glenda
	Gough, Laura	Griffin, Caroline
	Grimes, Claire	Heffernan, Paula
	Hobbs, Sarah	Houlihan, Nuala
	Hyland, Jacintha	Jarrett, Mary
	Kavanagh, Sinead	Keating, Jean
	Kehoe, Mary	Kennington, Ruth
	Kilduff, Ciara	Kindlon, Deirdre
	Lacey, Bairbre	Lawlor, Emma
	Lennon, Ingrid	Maher, Susan
	Mann, Michelle	Mann, Nadine
	Martin, Heidee	McCormack, Niamh
	McDermott, Michelle	McElroy, Felicity
	McEntee, Clodagh	McGovern, Niamh
	McLoughlin, Ciara	McMahon, Averil
	Moloney, Laura	Moody, Ann Marie
1999	Mooney, Sarah	Moran, Aoife
	Moran, Ruth	Mullaney, Erica
	Murray, Aideen	Murray, Hazel
	Neligan, Sarah	O'Brien, Feena
	O'Connell, Elizabeth	O'Keeffe, Ciara
	O'Leary, Jean	O'Neill, Gemma
	O'Regan, Caitriona	O'Rourke, Emma
	O'Sullivan, Donna	Phillips, Carol Anne
	Pickett, Alison	Power, Lesley
	Reilly, Amanda	Rooney, Eimear
	Ryan, Lesley	Ryan, Siobhain
	Ryan, Suzanne	Smyth, Christina
	Swayne, Emma	Thompson, Juliannne
	Toner, Sinead	Tyrrell, Emma

YEAR	Students	
1999	Whelan, Sinead	Mitton, Louise
2000	Barry, Gillian	Bell, Niamh
	Blake, Gillian	Bolger, Samantha
	Bowler, Maeve	Brady, Sarah-Jane
	Brennan, Lorna	Brocklebank, Ciara
	Brown, Rosemarie	Buckley, Suzanne
	Byrne, Jillian	Byrne, Laura
	Canavan, Maria	Carolan, Fiona
	Carter, Rebecca	Carty, Ciara
	Carville, Julia	Chadwick, Linda
	Cooney, Gemma	Coyle, Emer
	Crowley, Sarah	Cullen, Alexandra
	Devaney, Janice	Devitt, Shaneen
	Dockrell, Claire	Donegan, Trevi
	Downes, Orla	Dunphy, Emma
	Farrell, Jennifer	Faughnan, Emer
	Fay, Isabelle	Field, Aoife
	Fitzgerald, Barbara	Fitzgerald, Jane
	Flanagan, Grainne	Garvey, Suzanne
	Gaynor, Karen	Guinnigle, Sinead
	Gunn, Emily	Hammond, Alva
	Hansberry, Susan	Hayes, Rhian Eleanor
	Hegarty, Aine	Heverin, Erica
	Hughes, Denise	Hughes, Laura
	Keany, Sheena	Kenny, Marcia
	Kernaghan, Fiona	King, Clare
	Kinsella, Mary Rose	Kirk, Erin Anne
	Lambert, Victoria	Lau, Ka Man
	Lynch, Joanne	Lynch, Niamh
	Lynch, Niamh	Mac Donnell, Lorna
	Maguire, Shona	Maher, Laura
	Mantout, Solange	Marnane, Orlagh
	McCarthy, Kate	McCormack, Ann

165

YEAR	**Students**	
2000	McGrath, Marilyn	McNerney, Eimear
	McPartland, Eimear	Meyler, Sarah
	Mitton, Louise Mary	Moore, Jennifer
	Moran, Susan	Moriarty, Laura
	Moss, Susan	Mulrooney, Jennifer
	Noone, Aoife	O'Brien, Aveen
	O'Callaghan, Emily	O'Connor, Katie
	O'Dowd, Jennifer	O'Grady, Petria
	O'Hara, Eimear	O'Neill, Emma
	O'Neill, Sarah	O'Reilly, Emma
	O'Riordan, Elaine	O'Sullivan, Grace
	Porter, Eberechi Marie	Powell, Mary
	Quinn, Laura Lee	Quinn, Nicola
	Rafter, Pamela	Rickard, Sarah
	Ross, Geraldine	Sharpe, Jennifer
	Shaughnessy, Rachel	Skelly, Claire
	Tierney, Orlaith	Ward, Eveleen
	Wheatley, Louise	Wynne, Karen
2001	Ali, Azka	Asaa, Holly
	Bolger, Susan	Boylan, Vivienne
	Brady, Ciara	Buggy, Yvonne
	Byrne, Laura	Byrne, Michelle
	Callaghan, Sorcha	Cheng, Qian
	Clarke, Mari-Claire	Claxton, Sinead
	Connellan, Grace	Cooke, Anna Marie
	Cousins, Susan	Crotty, Robin
	Cuffe, Brenda	Dempsey, Carol
	Doherty, Ailbhe	Doherty, Nuala
	Donnelly, Aoife	Doogan, Alana
	Dowling, Louise	Downes, Jane

YEAR	Students

2001

Drennan, Gemma	Farrelly, Grace
Farrelly, Jennifer	Fay, Josephine
Field, Sinead	Flamme, Alexandra
Gibson, Emma-Louise	Gilhawley, Fiona
Glennon, Fiona	Good, Oonagh
Heffernan, Anne	Henehan, Roisin
Ho, Siew Ping	Hourican, Niamh
Ibanez, Berta	Ibanez, Emma
Ingram, Monica	Kane, Leona
Kavanagh, Joyce	Kelleher, Finola
Kelly, Eadaoin	Kelly, Eimear
Kelly, Sarah	Kirk, Shannon
Koltachova, Evgenia	Lawlor, Sarah
Lennon, Niamh	Leonard, Clare
Lynch, Nollaig Anna	Lyons, Emma
Masterson, Fiona	McCabe, Cathriona
McCallion, Sarah	McCaughley, Claire
McEvitt, Barbara	McGoldrick, Lynne
McGrotty, Suzanne	McIntyre, Denise Anne
McKeon, Claire Susan	McKernan, Jennifer
Memery, Joanne	Moran, Ellen
Moran, Jennifer	Mulcahy, Kate
Mulrooney, Miriam	Murray, Joanna
Nally, Aoife	Noone, Ann Marie
Ní Choiléin, Lisa	O'Dowd, Kate
O'Loughlin, Nadine	O'Neill, Kate
O'Neill, Laura	Parlour, Anne Marie
Prenderville, Catherine	Riordan, Maeve
Ross, Rebecca	Russell-Hill, Paula
Sharkey, Lisa	Shaw, Jennifer
Smith, Caroline	Tierney, Caoimhe
Tynan, Sarah	

YEAR	Students

2002		
	Arkins, Cathy	Barnes, Mary
	Becker, Michelle	Brannigan, Emma
	Brennan, Niamh	Buckmaster, Aideen
	Byrne, Andrea	Byrne, Emma
	Campbell, Martina	Collins, Helen
	Colreavy, Michelle	Corr, Michelle
	Cosgrove, Sinead	Coyle, Emily
	Daly, Sandra	Dardis, Susan
	Davis, Yvonne	Davy, Stephanie
	Dawson, Louise	De Lacy, Claire
	Donnan, Sarah-Jane	Donohoe, Claire
	Doyle, Aimee	Doyle, Orlagh
	Duffy, Cliona	Fagan, Jennifer
	Farrelly, Carol	Fenton, Helen
	Foley, Denise	Freeman, Marie
	Gallagher, Yvonne	Gayer, Ann Marie
	Geday, Natalie	Gough, Susan
	Grey, Sarah	Hallahan, Roisin
	Hannon, Catherine	Hartigan, Sarah
	Healy, Kate	Heffernan, Siobhan
	Hennessy, Sinead	Hynes, Elaine
	Kelly, Patricia	Kidd, Jennifer
	Lawlor, Ciara	Lawlor, Melissa
	McCarthy, Louise	McCarthy, Paula-Jean
	McGinn, Aedin	McHale, Laura
	Meehan, Stephanie	Meyler, Linda
	Moloney, Suzanne	Monaghan, Ruth
	Murray, Charlene	Murray, Lucy
	Murtagh, Kate Louise	Neligan, Mary Louise
	Newham, Caitriona	O'Dea, Aisling
	O'Brien, Michelle	O'Keeffe, Jennifer
	O'Loughlin, Catriona	O'Neill, Rachel
	O'Reilly, Deirdre	O'Reilly, Marianne
	O'Shaughnessy, Michelle	Patten, Ruth

YEAR	Students	
2002	Poole, Deirdre	Rafter, Suzanne
	Reddin, Sarah	Rooney, Jennifer
	Rutledge, Gillian	Ryan, Kira
	Salmon, Aine	Sammon, Aoife
	Sexton, Gemma	Sheehan, Christina
	Smith, Allyson	Walsh, Anna
2003	Anderson, Laura	Beechinor, Orla
	Bourke, Joanna	Boylan, Ruth
	Brady, Lynne	Browne, Erika
	Burke, Lisa	Byrne, Siobhan
	Carberry, Rachel	Cockram, Maria
	Coleman, Fiona	Condren, Ruth
	Connolly, Michelle	Cullen, Rebecca
	Cummins, Naomi	Cummins, Orlaith
	Curley, Niamh	Demetriou, Anna Maria
	Donohue, Martina	Dromey, Linda
	Dunphy, Clare	Edwards, Cliodhna
	Felle, Eimear	Fitzgerald, Sinead
	Fleming, Gillian	Flynn, Lucy
	Flynn, Valerie	Fox, Sarah
	Freeman, Siobhan	Geraghty, Sarah
	Gildea-Byrne,	Good, Emily
	Greaney, Alicia	Hanley, Julie-Anne
	Hannifin, Avril	Harty, Adeline
	Hickey, Darina	Hogan, Derbhla
	Holmes, Suzanne	Hurney, Susann
	Hyland, Brionan	Irvine, Nicole
	Jolliffe, Melanie	Kavanagh, Aisling
	Kavanagh, Laura Jane	Keane, Sinead
	Keegan, Aoife	Kehoe, Claire
	Kelly, Danielle	Kelly, Mary

YEAR	Students

	Kirwan, Una	Liston, Jennifer
2003	Lyons, Katie	Malone, Leanne
	Malone, Orla	Mann, Samantha
	Martin, Lisa Marie	McAlinden, Ciara
	McAuley, Karen	McClean, Deirdre
	McKenna, Claire	McKernan, Laura
	McLaren, Aisling	McLaughlin, Maeve
	McLoughlin, Caoimhe	McMeel, Laura
	Monaghan, Caitriona	Mooney, Lisa
	Moriarty, Rachel	Mulcahy, Amy
	Munnelly, Aisling	Murphy, Orla
	Murray, Sheena	Nardone, Nadia
	Ni Chleirigh, Siobhan	Ni Shiothchain, Aisling
	Nolan Mirallecs, Sarah	Nolan, Jennifer
	O'Brien, Holly Ann	O'Brien, Sarah
	O'Connell, Jennifer	O'Connor, Sioda
	O'Halloran, Linda	O'Hara, Karen Ann
	O'Leary, Carolyn	O'Loughlin, Claire
	O'Malley, Eleanor	O'Neill, Catherine
	O'Neill, Susan	O'Regan, Paula
	O'Reilly, Jennifer	O'Sullivan, Lorna
	O'Toole, Martina	Parker, Jennifer
	Phelan, Louise	Prylowski, Lisa
	Purcell, Amy	Rearden, Katie Isobel
	Regazzoli, Michelle	Reilly, Jennifer
	Reynor, Amy	Ryan, Emma
	Ryan, Muireann	Stapleton, Emma
	Stokes, Emma Jane	Sweeney, Laragh
	Tang, Victoria	Walsh, Laura
	Walsh, Sarah	Ward, Melissa
2004	Adams, Claire	Akindolie, Karen
	Bailey, Niamh	Barnes, Emma
	Borza, Giovanna	Bradley, Maria

YEAR	Students

2004

Brady, Lyndsey	Brady, Sinead
Brennan, Ciara	Brogan, Julianne
Browne, Olivia	Cantwell, Eimear
Carroll, Brenda	Cassidy, Maria
Coughlan, Clare	Crummey, Patricia
Cummins, Zara	Doherty, Louise
Donnelly, Niamh	Dunne, Donna Marie
Dunning, Audrey	Ebbs, Amanda
Fagan, Veronica	Farrell, Amy
Farrell, Caoimhe	Farrell, Michelle
Farrell, Niamh	Farrelly, Helena
Farrelly, Thalita	Feeney, Jessica
Fitzsimons, Anna	Foley, Aoife
Foley, Ciara	Foley, Maeve
Freeman, Aislinne	Gantley, Aimée Marie
Gibson, Audrey	Goucher, Rebecca
Gough, Grace	Gray, Vivienne
Hafeez, Omarah	Hanley, Mary Anne
Hannon, Michelle	Heeney, Nicole
Heffernan, Sarah	Hussey, Leigh
Igoe, Jane	Keane, Dervla
Kelly, Ailbhe	Kelly, Aoife
Kelly, Lisa	Kenny, Aoife
Kenny, Helen	Kidd, Laura
King, Jennie	Kinsella, Michelle
Kirby, Máiréad	Lalor, Gillian
Laverty, Sarah	Lawlor, Emma
Leonard, Helen	Lombard, Katie
Malone, Tracy	Mansoor, Nazish
Marks, Rebecca	McDermott, Lucy
McGinn, Ciara	McKeon, Lisa
McKernan, Kate	Meehan, Laura

YEAR	Students	
2004	Molloy, Ríona	Moore, Jennifer
	Moran, Eileen	Moran, Emma
	Moriarty, Sarah	Morris, Aoife
	Noble, Sarah	O'Brien, Pamela
	O'Connor, Lydia	O'Connor, Niamh
	O'Donoghue, Jennifer	O'Flaherty, Maeve
	O'Hara, Kelly	O'Leary, Louise
	O'Malley, Orla	O'Reilly, Claire
	O'Reilly, Olivia-Jean	O'Toole, Fiona
	Phelan, Sarah-Jane	Quigley, Caroline
	Quigley, Niamh	Rahill, Louise
	Redmond, Sinead	Robinson, Rebecca
	Ruddle, Christina	Ryan, Louise
	Scannell, Shauna	Shaughnessy, Ciara
	Shaw, Danielle	Shields, Elaine
	Smith, Deirdre	Smyth, Katie
	Teehan, Caroline	Tsang, Alice
	Turner, Geraldine	Xu, Fei-Fei

Europe: 100 houses
935 Sisters

1807	France	47	houses
1854	Italy	2	houses
1860	Ireland	7	houses
1879	Scotland	3	houses
1881	Portugal	26	houese
1903	England	1	house
1903	Spain	12	houses
1912	Switzerland	1	house
1992	Poland	1	house

America: 78 houses
366 Sisters

1822	Guyana	3	houses
1822	Guadeloupe	8	houses
1822	Martinique	2	houses
1826	St. P. & Miquelon	2	houses
1836	Trinidad, Tobago	8	houses
1854	St. Lucia	1	house
1856	St. Vincent	2	houses
1864	Haiti	15	houses
1870	Peru	11	houses
1875	Grenada	2	houses
1947	U.S.A.	6	houses
1958	Canada	1	houses
1960	Brazil	9	houses
1967	Paraguay	4	houses
1993	Dominica	1	house
1997	Cuba	2	houses
2001	Argentina	1	house

Asia: 117 houses
981 Sisters

INDIA

1827	Pondicherry	13	houses
1861	West Bengal	20	houses
1894	Tamilnadu	43	houses
1948	Karnataka	11	houses
1963	Goa	4	houses
1971	Kerala	3	houses
1973	Sikkim	5	houses
1975	Jharkhand	2	houses
1982	Andhra	8	houses
1988	Bihar	1	house
1990	Delhi	1	house
1997	Assam	1	house
1988	Nepal	3	houses
1994	Philippines	2	houses

Oceania: 22 houses
98 Sisters

1844	Tahiti	4	houses
1847	Marquesas	1	house
1860	New Caledonia	2	houses
1888	Fiji	3	houses
1895	Cook Islands	1	house
1925	Raiatea	1	house
1940	New Zealand	4	houses
1950	Australia	4	houses
1970	Papua New Guinea	2	houses

Indian Ocean: 34 houses
197 Sisters

1817	Reunion	11	houses
1841	Small Islands of Madagascar	17	houses
1861	Seychelles	6	houses

Africa: 73 houses
357 Sisters

1818	Senegal	ᴿ10	houses
1822	Sierra Leone	4	houses
1822	Gambia	4	houses
1883	Angola	24	houses
1886	Congo	3	houses
1890	Mozambique	6	houses
1893	Guinea	5	houses
1966	Gabon	2	houses
1990	Ghana	2	houses
1993	Guinea Bissau	2	houses
1993	R.D. of Congo	2	houses
1995	Cameroon	5	houses
1997	Tanzania	2	houses
1999	Nigeria	2	houses

The 1st column indicates the date of foundation in the country or State

List of Communities

173

FORM G.—COLLEGE AND BOARDING SCHOOL RETURN.

No. on Form B. 73

County, _Dublin_ | Parliamentary Division, _Nth. Dubl._ | Poor Law Union, _Nth. Dublin_ | District Electoral Division _Castleknock_ | Townland _Castleknock_ | Barony, _Castleknock_ | Parish _Cas_

Parliamentary Borough, / | City, / | Urban District, / | Town, / | Street, v

RETURN of the Masters (except the Principals or Proprietors), Teachers, and Students or Pupils who slept or abode in the College of

or the Boarding School of _Mount Sackville Convent_ at _Castleknock_ on the Night of Sunday, the 31st of March, 1901, and of those who arrived on Monday, the April, who were not enumerated elsewhere.

No.	Christian Name	Surname	Religious Profession	Education	Age	Sex	Rank, Profession or standing	Marriage	Where Born	Irish Language	If Deaf and Dumb, etc.
60	Mary	Burke	Roman Catholic	Read & write	18	F	Pupil	Not married	Co. Tipperary		
61	Mary Kate	Butler	R. Catholic	Read & write	16	F	Pupil		Co. Wexford Enniscorthy		
62	Annie	Flynn	R. Catholic	Read & write	16	F	Pupil		Co. Meath		
63	Elizabeth	Gunning	R. Catholic	Read & write	16	F	Pupil		King's Co.		
64	Mary Jane	Blake	R. Catholic	Read & write	15	F	Pupil		Co. Galway		
65	Margaret	Mulligany	R. Catholic	Read & write	15	F	Pupil		Carlow		
66	Mary Ann	Moylan	R. Catholic	Read & write	15	F	Pupil		Co. Tipperary		
67	Monica	Jordan	R. Catholic	Read & write	14	F	Pupil		Co. Galway		
68	Elizabeth	Connolly	R. Catholic	Read & write	14	F	Pupil		Cong		
69	Helena	O'Neill	R. Catholic	Read & write	14	F	Pupil		Kildare		
70	Elizabeth	Sheridan	R. Catholic	Read & write	14	F	Pupil		Co. Meath		
71	Mary Cathne	Gallagher	R. Catholic	Read & write	13	F	Pupil		Co. Donegal		
72	Bridget	Mahon	R. Catholic	Read & write	13	F	Pupil		Dublin City		
73	Kate	Kelly	R. Catholic	Read & write	13	F	Pupil		Tipperary		
74	Maria	Allen	R. Catholic	Read & write	13	F	Pupil		Co. East Meath		
75	Nora	Maloney	R. Catholic	Read & write	13	F	Pupil		Tipperary Co.		
76	Kathleen	Murphy	R. Catholic	Read & write	13	F	Pupil		Co. Galway		
77	Mary	Sheridan	R. Catholic	Read & write	13	F	Pupil		Co. Meath		
78	Annie	Sheridan	R. Catholic	Read & write	12	F	Pupil		Co. Meath		
79	Margaret	Dee	R. Catholic	Read & write	12	F	Pupil		Co. Tipperary		
80	Eva	O'Neill	R. Catholic	Read & write	12	F	Pupil		Dublin City		
81	Winifred	Jordan	R. Catholic	Read & write	12	F	Pupil		Co. Galway		
82	Ellen	Doolan	R. Catholic	Read & write	12	F	Pupil		Wexford		
83	Mary	Connolly	R. Catholic	Read & write	12	F	Pupil		Co. Galway		
84	Mary	Sexton	R. Catholic	Read & write	11	F	Pupil		Co. Dublin		
85	Gertrude	Gibbons	R. Catholic	Read & write	11	F	Pupil				
86	Mary Jane	Byrne	R. Catholic	Read & write	11	F	Pupil				
87	M. Margaret	Roche	R. Catholic	Read & write	10	F	Pupil				
	Philomena	Connolly	R. Catholic	Read & write	10	F	Pupil		Co. Galway		
	Johanna	O'Neill	R. Catholic	Read & write	9	F	Pupil		Cork City		
	Bridget	Flurry	R. Catholic	Read & write	9	F	Pupil		Co. Galway		
		Connolly	R. Catholic	Read & write	9	F	Pupil		Co. Galway		
		Roche	R. Catholic	Read & write	9	F	Pupil				
	Kathleen	O'Connor	R. Catholic	Read & write	9	F	Pupil		Dublin City		
			R. Catholic	Read & write	8	F	Pupil				

Census Dublin 1901, Castleknock Townland, 21/6, Forms A & G73

No.	Christian Name	Surname	Religious Profession	Education	Age	Sex	Rank, Profession or standing	Marriage	Where Born	Irish Language	If Deaf &c.
36	Mary	Donlon	R. Catholic	Read & write	23	F.	Pupil	Not married	King's Co.		
37	Mary Josephine	Mulvihy	R. Catholic	Read & write	22	F.	Pupil	Not married	Co. Galway		
38	Julia	Dooling	R. Catholic	Read & write	21	F.	Pupil	Not married	King's Co.		
39	Mary Ann	Davey	R. Catholic	Read & write	19	F.	Pupil	Not married	King's Co.		
40	Mary	Guinan	R. Catholic	Read & write	18	F.	Pupil	Not married	King's Co.		
41	Ellen	Hickey	R. Catholic	Read & write	18	F.	Pupil	Not married	Co. Cork		
42	Ellen	O'Donnell	R. Catholic	Read & write	18	F.	Pupil	Not married	Co. Tipperary		
43	Maretta	Byrne	R. Catholic	Read & write	18	F.	Pupil	Not married	King's Co.		
44	Margaret	Nolan	R. Catholic	Read & write	17	F.	Pupil	Not married	King's Co.		
45	Agatha	Ryan	R. Catholic	Read & write	17	F.	Pupil	Not married	Co. Kilkenny		
46	Bridget	Mc Tiernay	R. Catholic	Read & write	24	F.	Pupil	Not married	Co. Cavan		
47	Sara	Connell	R. Catholic	Read & write	20	F.	Pupil		Kilbeggan		
48	Mary Kate	Dee	R. Catholic	Read & write	19	F.	Pupil		Bansha		
49	Winifred	Dee	R. Catholic	Read & write	17	F.	Pupil		Bansha		
50	Ellie	Barragry	R. Catholic	Read & write	17	F.	Pupil		Oola Co. Lim.		
51	Lizzie	Wyatt	R. Catholic	Read & write	17	F.	Pupil		Thomas		
52	Mary	Hughes	R. Catholic	Read & write	17	F.	Pupil		Cong Co. Mayo		
53	Mabel	Fahi	R. Catholic	Read & write	17	F.	Pupil		Rush		
54	Elizabeth	Doolan	R. Catholic	Read & write	16	F.	Pupil		Frankford		
55	Kate	Mc Weller	R. Catholic	Read & write	16	F.	Pupil		Dummore		
56	Ellie	Kavanagh	R. Catholic	Read & write	16	F.	Pupil		Borris		
57	Julia	O'Donnell	R. Catholic	Read & write	18	F.	Pupil		Tipperary		
58	Maggie	Rowan	R. Catholic	Read & write	18	F.	Pupil		Kilbeggan		
59	Ann Agnes	Gibbons	R. Catholic	Read & write	15	F.	Pupil		Glenamoe		

The foregoing Return, consisting of 2 sheets, relating to the Masters, Teachers and Students or Pupils in this Institution, is correct, according to the best of my knowledge and bel

Signature of Head of Institution _Agatha Shee_
Date _12th April 19_

I hereby certify, as required by the Act 63 Vic. c. 6, s. 6 (1), that the foregoing Return is correct, according to the best of my knowledge and belief.

Michl Harrison Con Signature of Enumer

6th April 1901 Date.

Approved,
D. HARREL,
Dublin Castle.
21st December, 1900.

ROBERT E. MATHESON,
Registrar-General,
T. J. BELLINGHAM BRADY,
ROBERT J. KREW
Commissioners.

Census Dublin 1901, Castleknock Townland, 21/6, Forms A & G73

175

FORM G.—COLLEGE AND BOARDING SCHOOL RETURN.

No. on Form B. __ 7

County, _Dublin_ Parliamentary Division, _North Dublin_ Poor Law Union, _North Dublin_ District Electoral Division, _Castleknock_ Townland _Castleknock_ Barony, _Castlek._ Parish, _C_

Parliamentary Borough, _____ City, _____ Urban District, ✓ Town, ✓ Street, ·

RETURN of the Masters (except the Principals or Proprietors), Teachers, and Students or Pupils who slept or abode in the College of _____ at _____

or the Boarding School of _Mount Sackville Convent_ at _Castleknock_ on the Night of Sunday, the 31st of March, 1901, and of those who arrived on Monday the April, who were not enumerated elsewhere.

In filling these Returns, pray observe the Instructions given on "Form A"—The Family Return.

NOTE—The Principals or Proprietors of Colleges and Boarding Schools are, with their Families and Servants, to be returned not on this Form, but on "Form A."

	Christian Name	Surname	Religious Profession	Education	Age (Years)	Sex	Rank, Profession or standing	Marriage	Where Born	Irish Language	If Deaf and Dumb, &c.
1	Margaret	Foulon	Roman Catholic	Read & write	12	F	Manual labour	Not married	Co. Carlow		
2	Ellen	Power	R. Catholic	Read & write	63	F	Teacher	Not married	Co. Waterford		
3	Ann	Flynn	R. Catholic	Read & write	65	F	Manual labour	Not married	Co. Mayo	Irish & English	
4	Margaret	Crowley	R. Catholic	Read & write	56	F	Teacher	Not married	Co. Kilkenny		
5	Mary Ellen	Fay	R. Catholic	Read & write	53	F	Teacher	Not married	England		
6	Kate	Carroll	R. Catholic	Read & write	52	F	Teacher	Not married	Co. Cavan		
7	Marie	Jacquet	R. Catholic	Read & write	52	F	Teacher	Not married	France		
8	Nora	Moloney	R. Catholic	Read & write	41	F	Teacher	Not married	Co. Clare		
9	Ellen	McCormack	R. Catholic	Read & write	41	F	Teacher	Not married	Co. Tipperary		
10	Kate	Moylan	R. Catholic	Read & write	41	F	Teacher	Not married	Co. Tipperary		
11	Kate	Woods	R. Catholic	Read & write	41	F	Manual labour	Not married	England		
12	Mary	O'Rourke	R. Catholic	Read & write	40	F	Manual labour	Not married	King's Co.		
13	Patricia	Reigh	R. Catholic	Read & write	37	F	Manual labour	Not married	Germany		
14	Elizabeth	Sweeney	R. Catholic	Read & write	37	F	Teacher	Not married	Co. Donegal		
15	Margaret	O'Connell	R. Catholic	Read & write	34	F	Manual labour	Not married	Co. Clare		
16	Mary	Donnelly	R. Catholic	Read & write	34	F	Teacher	Not married	Co. Dublin		
17	Jane	Sockman	R. Catholic	Read & write	33	F	Teacher	Not married	Co. Dublin		
18	Marie Jeanne	Ezekiri	R. Catholic	Read & write	32	F	Manual labour	Not married	France		
19	Marie Louise	Fay	R. Catholic	Read & write	31	F	Manual labour	Not married	Germany		
20	Margaret Ellen	McDermott	R. Catholic	Read & write	30	F	Teacher	Not married	England		
21	Mary	Coghlan	R. Catholic	Read & write	29	F	Teacher	Not married	Co. Clare		
22	Natalie	Delort	R. Catholic	Read & write	29	F	Manual labour	Not married	France		
23	Marie	Deringer	R. Catholic	Read & write	28	F	Teacher	Not married	Germany		
24	Mary	Cunningham	R. Catholic	Read & write	28	F	Teacher	Not married	Co. Galway		
25	Bridget	Dorlan	R. Catholic	Read & write	27	F	Teacher	Not married	King's Co.		
26	Josephine	Dobs	R. Catholic	Read & write	31	F	Manual labour	Not married	Germany		
27	Winifred	O'Connell	R. Catholic	Read & write	26	F	Teacher	Not married	Limerick		
28	Marie Rose	Gazes	R. Catholic	Read & write	25	F	Manual labour	Not married	France		
29	Catherine	Walshe	R. Catholic	Read & write	31	F	Manual labour	Not married	Co. Tipperary		
30	Grace	_____	R. Catholic	Read & write	22	F	Teacher	Not married	Co. Kild.		
31	Hannah	O'Brien	R. Catholic	Read & write	29	F	Pupil	Not married	Co. Cork		
	Mary	Somers	R. Catholic	Read & write	28	F	Pupil	Not married	Co. Limerick		
	Mary	Garry	R. Catholic	Read & write	26	F	Pupil	Not married	Co. Clare		
	Catherine	Reilly	R. Catholic	Read & write	21	F	Pupil	Not married	Co. West Meath		
	Morgan	McRowles	R. Catholic	Read & write	26	F	Pupil	Not married	King's Co.		

Census Dublin 1901, Castleknock Townland, 21/6, Forms A & G73

No.	Name and Surname.		Religious Profession.	Education.	Age.		Sex.	Rank, Profession or standing.	Marriage.	Where Born.	Irish Language.	If Deaf and Dumb...
	Christian Name.	Surname.			Years, on last Birth-day.	Write "M" for Males and "F" for Females.		State Rank in the Institution—whether Fellow, Professor, Teacher, or Student or Pupil.	Whether "Married," "Widower," "Widow," or "not Married."	If in Ireland, state in what County or City; if elsewhere, state the name of the Country		
	Mary	O'Keefe	Roman Catholic	Read & write	8		F	Pupil	Not married	Co. Dublin		
	Margaret M.	Thornton	R. Catholic	Read & write	8		F	Pupil		Dublin city		
	Kathleen	O'Connor	R. Catholic	Read & write	8		F	Pupil		Dublin city		
	Gertrude	Connolly	R. Catholic	Read & write	7		F	Pupil		Co. Galway		
	Eva	O'Ball	R. Catholic	Read & write	7		F	Pupil		London		
	Mary Agnes	Thornton	R. Catholic	Read & write	7		F	Pupil		Dublin city		
	Frances	O'Ball	R. Catholic	Read & write	1		F	Pupil		Dublin city		
2	Josephine	Thornton	R. Catholic	Read & write	1		F	Pupil		Dublin city		
3	Mary	Ballady	R. Catholic	Read & write	1		F	Pupil		Co. Dublin		
4	Mary	Rose	R. Catholic	Read & write	6		F	Pupil		Dublin city		
5	Bridget	Sullivan	R. Catholic	Read & write	11		F	Pupil		Limerick Co.		

The foregoing Return, consisting of ... relating to the Masters, Teachers, and Students or Pupils in this Institution, is correct, according to the best of my knowledge and belief.

Signature of Head of Institution _____

Date _____

I hereby certify, as required by the Act ... that the foregoing Return is correct, according to the best of my knowledge and belief.

Census Dublin 1901, Castleknock Townland, 21/6, Forms A & G73

177

CENSUS OF IRELAND, 1911.

Two Examples of the mode of filling up this Table are given on the other side.

FORM A.

No. on Form B.

RETURN of the MEMBERS of this FAMILY and their VISITORS, BOARDERS, SERVANTS, &c., who slept or abode in this House on the night of SUNDAY, the 2nd of APRIL, 1911.

No.	NAME AND SURNAME		RELATION to Head of Family	RELIGIOUS PROFESSION	EDUCATION	AGE (last Birthday) and SEX		RANK, PROFESSION, OR OCCUPATION	PARTICULARS AS TO MARRIAGE				WHERE BORN	IRISH LANGUAGE	If Deaf, Dumb, &c.
	Christian Name	Surname				Ages of Males	Ages of Females		Whether Married, Widower, Widow, or Single	Completed years the present Marriage has lasted	Children born alive	Children still living			
	1	2	3	4	5	6		7	8	9	10	11	12	13	14
1		Browne	Boarder	Roman Catholic	Read & write	43			Single				Co. Galway		
2		Browne		Roman Catholic		42			Single				Co. Dublin		
3		Browne		Roman Catholic		41			Single				Kings Co.		
4		Browne		Roman Catholic		43			Single				Co. Galway		
5		Browne		Roman Catholic		39			Single				Co. Galway		
6		Browne		Roman Catholic		36			Single				Co. Kildare		
7		Browne		Roman Catholic		35			Single				Co. Limerick		
8		Browne		Roman Catholic		33			Single				Co. Louth		
9		Browne		Roman Catholic		32			Single				Co. Clare		
10		Browne		Roman Catholic		30			Single				Co. Clare		
11		Browne		Roman Catholic		27			Single				Co. Wexford		

I hereby certify, as required by the Act 10 Edw. VII, and 1 Geo. V, cap. 11, that the foregoing Return, if correct, according to the best of my knowledge and belief.

_____ Signature of Enumerator.

I believe the foregoing to be a true Return.

_____ Signature of Head of Family.

Census Dublin 1911, Castleknock Townland, 24/6/1, Forms A & G40

CENSUS OF IRELAND, 1911.

Two Examples of the mode of filling up this Table are given on the other side.

FORM A.

No. on Form B. _____

RETURN of the MEMBERS of this FAMILY and their VISITORS, BOARDERS, SERVANTS, &c., who slept or abode in this House on the night of SUNDAY, the 2nd of APRIL, 1911.

No.	NAME AND SURNAME — Christian Name	Surname	RELATION to Head of Family	RELIGIOUS PROFESSION	EDUCATION	AGE (last Birthday) and SEX — Males	Females	RANK, PROFESSION, OR OCCUPATION	PARTICULARS AS TO MARRIAGE — Whether "Married," "Widower," "Widow," or "Single"	Completed years the present Marriage has lasted	Children born alive — Total Children born alive	Children still living	WHERE BORN	IRISH LANGUAGE
1	Henry	Bolton	Head	Roman Catholic	Read & write	26		Manu	Single				Dublin	
2	Dorothea	Bolton		Roman Catholic	Read & write	28		Manu	Single				Dublin	
3	Hugh			Roman Catholic	Read & write	30 71		Manu	Single				Kings County	Irish English
4	Mary			Roman Catholic	Read & write	49		Manu	Single				Galway	
5	Ellen			Roman Catholic	Read & write	56		Manu	Single				Galway	
6	Mary			Roman Catholic	Read & write	49		Manu	Single				Co. Kilkenny	
7	Anne			Roman Catholic	Read & write	47		Manu	Single				Co. Tipperary	
8	Margaret			Roman Catholic	Read & write	46		Manu	Single				Co. Monaghan	
9	Mary Anne	Connell		Roman Catholic	Read & write	44		Manu	Single				Co. Clare	
10	Mary Jane	Miller		Roman Catholic	Read & write	43		Manu	Single				Co. Galway	
11	Frances Josephine	Rose Silver		Roman Catholic	Read & write	40		Manu	Single				Co. Mayo	
12	Dorothea	Gillen		Roman Catholic	Read & write	38		Manu	Single				Galway	
13	Josephine	Gillen		Roman Catholic	Read & write	39		Manu	Single				Francie	
14	Josephine	Gibbs		Roman Catholic	Read & write	36		Manu	Single				alive Sing	
15	Mary Norma	A Cork		Roman Catholic	Read twice	35		Manu	Single				Galway France	

I hereby certify, as required by the Act 10 Edw. VII., and 1 Geo. V., cap. 11, that the foregoing Return is correct, according to the best of my knowledge and belief.

H. Gossett. _____ Signature of Enumerator.

I believe the foregoing to be a true Return.

Dorothea Bolton _____ Signature of Head of Family.

CENSUS OF IRELAND, 1911.

Two Examples of the mode of filling up this Table are given on the other side.

FORM A.

No. on Form B.

RETURN of the MEMBERS of this FAMILY and their VISITORS, BOARDERS, SERVANTS, &c., who slept or abode in this House on the night of SUNDAY, the 2nd of APRIL, 1911.

Number.	NAME AND SURNAME		RELATION to Head of Family	RELIGIOUS PROFESSION	EDUCATION	AGE (last Birthday) and SEX		RANK, PROFESSION, OR OCCUPATION	PARTICULARS AS TO MARRIAGE				WHERE BORN	IRISH LANGUAGE
	Christian Name	Surname				Ages Males	Ages Females							
1	Agatha	Hewer	Superioress	Roman Catholic	Read and Write		53	Nun	Single				County Carlow	
2	Elizabeth	Sherwood	Sisters	Roman Catholic	Read and Write		49	Nun	Single				Co. Donegal	Irish & English
3	Ellen	Power	"	Roman Catholic	Read and Write		71	Nun	Single				Co. Dublin	
4	Margaret	Fay	"	Roman Catholic	Read and Write		65	Nun	Single				Co. Westmeath	
5	Catharine	Fay	"	Roman Catholic	Read and Write		62	Nun	Single				Co. Kildare	
6	Catharine	Conroy	"	Roman Catholic	Read and Write		61	Nun	Single				Co. Clare	
7	Susanna	Laragan	"	Roman Catholic	Read and Write		61	Nun	Single				France	
8	Marianne	Keogh	"	Roman Catholic	Read and Write		58	Nun	Single				Co. Dublin	
9	Anne	Doherty	"	Roman Catholic	Read and Write		58	Nun	Single				Co. Derry	
10	Mary Anne	Hughes	"	Roman Catholic	Read and Write		57	Nun	Single				Co. Tipperary	
11	Kate	Carey	"	Roman Catholic	Read and Write		50	Nun	Single				Kilkenny	
12	Ellen	Clarendon	"	Roman Catholic	Read and Write		50	Nun	Single				Co. Tipperary	
13	Mary	Stephens	"	Roman Catholic	Read and Write		48	Nun	Single				Co. Cork	
14	Bridget	Conroy	"	Roman Catholic	Read and Write		47	Nun	Single				Carlow	
15	Margaret Anne	Mulholland	"	Roman Catholic	Read and Write		45	Nun	Single				Co. Fermanagh	

I hereby certify, as required by the Act 10 Edw. VII., and 1 Geo. V., cap. 11, that the foregoing Return is correct, according to the best of my knowledge and belief.

M. Maguire _____ Signature of Enumerator.

I believe the foregoing to be a true Return.

_____ Signature of Head of Family

Census Dublin 1911, Castleknock Townland, 24/6/1, Forms A & G40

CENSUS OF IRELAND, 1911.

Two Examples of the mode of filling up this Table are given on the other side.

FORM A.

RETURN of the MEMBERS of this FAMILY and their VISITORS, BOARDERS, SERVANTS, &c., who slept or abode in this House on the night of SUNDAY, the 2nd of APRIL, 1911.

No. on Form B.__

Number.	NAME AND SURNAME.		RELATION to Head of Family.	RELIGIOUS PROFESSION.	EDUCATION.	AGE (last Birthday) and SEX.		RANK, PROFESSION, OR OCCUPATION.	PARTICULARS AS TO MARRIAGE.				WHERE BORN.	IRISH LANGUAGE.
	Christian Name.	Surname.				Ages of Males.	Ages of Females.		Whether "Married," "Widower," "Widow," or "Single."	Completed years the present Marriage has lasted.	Total Children born alive.	Children still living.		
	1.	2.	3.	4.	5.	6.	7.	8.	9.	10.	11.	12.	13.	14.	15.
1	Sarah Josephine	Smith	Boarder	Roman Catholic	Read Write		16 chd		Widow		8	Three still Lvg	Dublin City	Customs	
2	Emily	Mulholland	Boarder	Roman Catholic	Read Write		68		Single				Customs	
3	Bridget	Jordan	Boarder	Roman Catholic	Read Write	76		Domestic Servant	Single				Co Lautrim	
4	Kate	Kelly	Servant	Roman Catholic	Read Write	32		Domestic Servant	Single				Co. Dublin	
5	Mary	Can	Servant	Roman Catholic	Read Write	30		Domestic Servant	Single				Dubli. City	
6	Sarah	Mc Loughlan	Servant	Roman Catholic	Read Write	33		Domestic Servant	Single				Co Down	
7	Mary	Brien	Servant	Roman Catholic	Read Write	27		Domestic Servant	Single				Co Dubli.	
8	Henry	Robinson	Servant	Roman Catholic	Read Write	17		Domestic Servant	Single				Co Dubli.	
9														
0														
1														
2														
3														
4														
5														

I hereby certify, as required by the Act 10 Edw. VII, and 1 Geo. V. cap. 11, that the foregoing Return is correct, according to the best of my knowledge and belief.

_____ Signature of Enumerator.

I believe the foregoing to be a true Return.

_____ Signature of Head of Family.

Census Dublin 1911, Castleknock Townland, 24/6/1, Forms A & G40

181

CENSUS OF IRELAND, 1911.

FORM C.—COLLEGE AND BOARDING SCHOOL RETURN.

No. on Form B.—

Parliamentary { A Dublin Poor Law } A Dublin District Electoral _____ Townland, _____ Barony, _____ Parish, _____
Division, { Union, } Division,

City, _____   Urban District, _____   Town, _____   Street, _____

of _____ at _____

sters (except the Principals or Proprietors), Teachers, and Students or Pupils who slept or abode in the College of _____, on the Night of Sunday, the 2nd of April, 1911, and of those who arrived on Monday, t

enumerated elsewhere.

NOTE.—The Principals or Proprietors of College and Boarding Schools are, with their Families and Servants, to be returned not on this Form, but on "Form A."

me and Surname	Religious Profession.	Education.	Age (last birthday) and Sex.		Rank, Profession or standing.	Marriage.	Where Born.	Irish Language.	If Deaf a
Surnames.			Ages of Males.	Ages of Females.					
Kennedy	Roman Catholic	Read & write	11		Pupil	Single	Co. Dublin		
Brown	Roman Catholic	Read & write	10		Pupil	Single	Co. Kildare		
Hear?	Roman Catholic	Read & write	10		Pupil	Single	Dublin City		
McDermott	Roman Catholic	Read & write	10		Pupil	Single	Co. Kilkenny		
Kelly	Roman Catholic	Read & write	10		Pupil	Single	Co. Dublin		
Hear?	Roman Catholic	Read & write	9		Pupil	Single	Co. Dublin		
McDermott	Roman Catholic	Read & write	9		Pupil	Single	Co. Kilkenny		
Raynor	Roman Catholic	Read & write	8		Pupil	Single	Africa Berg		
Cavan	Roman Catholic	Read & write	8		Pupil	Single	Dublin City		
William	Roman Catholic	Read & write	8		Pupil	Single	Co. Dublin		
Hear?	Roman Catholic	Read & write	7		Pupil	Single	Dublin City		
Kielan	Roman Catholic	Read & write	7		Pupil	Single	Co. Dublin		

Census Dublin 1911, Castleknock Townland, 24/6/1, Forms A & G40

CENSUS OF IRELAND 1911.

FORM G.—COLLEGE AND BOARDING SCHOOL RETURN.

No. on Form B

Parliamentary Division: *North Dublin* — Poor Law Union: *North Dublin* — District Electoral Division: *Castleknock* — Townland: *Castleknock* — Barony: *Castleknock*

City: ____ Urban District: ____ Town: ____ Street: ____

the Masters (except the Principals or Proprietors), Teachers, and Students or Pupils who slept or abode in the College of ____ at ____

ng School of *Mt Sackville Convent* at *Castleknock* ____ on the Night of Sunday, the 2nd of April, 1911, and of those who arrived on Mo:

ere not enumerated elsewhere. — ☞ In filling these Returns, pray observe the instructions given on "Form A"—The Family Return.

NOTE—The Principals or Proprietors of Colleges and Boarding Schools are, with their Families and Servants, to be returned not on this Form, but on "Form A."

Name and Surname		Religious Profession	Education	Age (last birthday) and Sex		Rank, Profession or standing	Marriage	Where Born	Irish Language
Christian Name	Surname			Age of Males	Age of Females				
gdalen May	Gallagher	Roman Catholic	Read and write		19	Pupil	Single	Co Donegal	
ne J.	O'Connor	Roman Catholic	Read and write		20	Pupil	Single	Co Kildare	Irish and English
ryet	Scanlan	Roman Catholic	Read + write		18	Pupil	Single	Co Dublin	Irish + English
yela	Brady	Roman Catholic	Read + write		18	Pupil	Single	Co Dublin	
eanor	Nolan	Roman Catholic	Read + write		17	Pupil	Single	Co Dublin	
ry Julia	O'Sullivan	Roman Catholic	Read + write		17	Pupil	Single	Co Dublin	
llie	Sheridan	Roman Catholic	Read + write		17	Pupil	Single	Co Westmeath	
any	Kennedy	Roman Catholic	Read + write		17	Pupil	Single	Co Tipperary	
arguet	Hoare	Roman Catholic	Read + write		16	Pupil	Single	Co Dublin	Irish + English
en Shope	Durnin	Roman Catholic	Read + write		16	Pupil	Single	Co Kildare	
gdalen M.	Donnelly	Roman Catholic	Read + write		16	Pupil	Single	Co Dublin	
____	Lorkin	Roman Catholic	Read + write		16	Pupil	Single	Co Clare	Irish + English
lice	Connolly	Roman Catholic	Read + write		16	Pupil	Single	Co Roscommon	
arguet	Harney	Roman Catholic	Read + write		16	Pupil	Single	Co Donegal	
race	O'Donnell	Roman Catholic	Read + write		16	Pupil	Single		
hanna	Fleming	Roman Catholic	Read + write		16	Pupil	Single	Co Tipperary	
inetta	Lewett	Roman Catholic	Read + write		16	Pupil	Single	New York USA	
arphine a	Moss	Roman Catholic	Read + write		15	Pupil	Single	Dublin City	
oreta	Hayden	Roman Catholic	Read + write		15	Pupil	Single	Co Cork	
____	Lally	Roman Catholic	Read + write		15	Pupil	Single		
nany	McSherry	Roman Catholic	Read + write		15	Pupil	Single	Co Armagh	
arguet E.	Walshe	Roman Catholic	Read + write		15	Pupil	Single	Co Waterford	
Ethel	O'Brien	Roman Catholic	Read + write		15	Pupil	Single	Co Dublin	
oephine	Donnelly	Roman Catholic	Read + write		14	Pupil	Single	Dublin City	
alfreda	O'Farrell	Roman Catholic	Read + write		15	Pupil	Single		

Census Dublin 1911, Castleknock Townland, 24/6/1, Forms A & G40

Form G.—College and Boarding School Return—continued.

Name and Surname.		Religious Profession.	Education.	Age (last birthday) and Sex.		Rank, Profession or standing.	Marriage.	Where Born.	Irish
Christian Name.	Surname.	State here the particular Religion, or Religious Denomination, to which each person belongs. (Members of Protestant Denominations should not be described by the vague term "Protestant," but the name of the particular Church, Denomination, or Body to which they belong should be entered.)	State here whether he or she can "Read and Write," can "Read" only, or "Cannot Read."	Ages of Males.	Ages of Females.	State Rank in the Institution—whether Fellow, Professor, Teacher, or Student or Pupil.	Whether "Married," "Widower," "Widow," or "Single."	If in Ireland, state in what County or City; if elsewhere, state the name of the Country.	
Mary	Finnegan	Roman Catholic	Read and write		13	Pupil	Single	Dublin City	
Louisa	Bowie	Roman Catholic	Read and write		13	Pupil	Single	Co Kildare	
Angela	Hoare	Roman Catholic	Read and write		13	Pupil	Single	Dublin City	
Elsie M.	McDermott	Roman Catholic	Read and write		13	Pupil	Single	Co Meath	
Mary	Dunne	Roman Catholic	Read and write		13	Pupil	Single	Co. Dublin	
Catherine	Fitzgerald	Roman Catholic	Read and write		12	Pupil	Single	Kings Co.	
Monica	O'Farrell	Roman Catholic	Read and write		12	Pupil	Single	Dublin City	
Emma	Kelly	Roman Catholic	Read and write		12	Pupil	Single	Co Roscommon	
Angela	Donnelly	Roman Catholic	Read and write		12	Pupil	Single	Dublin City	
Mary	Hamey	Roman Catholic	Read and write		11	Pupil	Single	Co. Galway	
Mary	Farrington	Roman Catholic	Read and write		11	Pupil	Single	Dublin City	
Nora	Harrington	Roman Catholic	Read and write		11	Pupil	Single	Dublin City	
Eva	Doyle	Roman Catholic	Read and write		11	Pupil	Single	Co Dublin	
Marie	Mulhall	Roman Catholic	Read and write		11	Pupil	Single	Dublin City	
Mary Rose	McDermott	Roman Catholic	Read and write		11	Pupil	Single	Co Meath	
Marjorie	Mulhall	Roman Catholic	Read and write		10	Pupil	Single	Dublin	
Norah	Hughes	Roman Catholic	Read and write		11	Pupil	Single	Co Galway	
Emily	Killen	Roman Catholic	Read and write		11	Pupil	Single	Co Dublin	
Elizabeth	Farrington	Roman Catholic	Read and write		10	Pupil	Single	Dublin City	
Kathleen	Reynor	Roman Catholic	Read and write		10	Pupil	Single	Co Dublin	
Laura	Neane	Roman Catholic	Read and write		9	Pupil	Single	Co Down	
Joy	Pemberton	Roman Catholic	Read and write		9	Pupil	Single	Co Dublin	
Lily	Pemberton	Roman Catholic	Read and write		8	Pupil	Single	Co. Dublin	
Margaret	McCarthy	Roman Catholic	Read and write		7	Pupil	Single	Co Cork	
Finola	Harrington	Roman Catholic	Cannot read		5	Pupil	Single	Dublin City	
Patrick E. A	Lawler	Roman Catholic	Read and write	12		Pupil	Single	Co Kildare	[1]
Joseph P.	Cregan	Roman Catholic	Read and write	12		Pupil	Single	Co Limerick	
Ralph J.	Bowie	Roman Catholic	Read and write	12		Pupil	Single	Co Kildare	
Michael A.	Walsh	Roman Catholic	Read and write	11		Pupil	Single	Queens Co.	
Cecil J.	Finnegan	Roman Catholic	Read and write	12		Pupil	Single	Dublin City	
Oliver A.	Kennedy	Roman Catholic	Read and write	12		Pupil	Single	Co Dublin	

Census Dublin 1911, Castleknock Townland, 24/6/1, Forms A & G40

184

Alice	Connolly	Roman Catholic	Read & write	16	Pupil	Single	Co Sligo
Margret	Harvey	Roman Catholic	Read & write	16	Pupil	Single	Co Roscom
Grace	O'Donnell	Roman Catholic	Read & write	16	Pupil	Single	Co Down
Johanna	Fleming	Roman Catholic	Read & write	16	Pupil	Single	Co Tipper
Annetta	Sewell	Roman Catholic	Read & write	16	Pupil	Single	New York
Josephine	Moss	Roman Catholic	Read & write	16	Pupil	Single	Co Meath
Loreta	Hayden	Roman Catholic	Read & write	15	Pupil	Single	Dublin C
Teresa Josie	Lally	Roman Catholic	Read & write	15	Pupil	Single	Co Cork
Mary	McSherry	Roman Catholic	Read & write	15	Pupil	Single	Co Down
Margret J.	Walshe	Roman Catholic	Read & write	15	Pupil	Single	Co Water
Ethel	O'Brien	Roman Catholic	Read & write	15	Pupil	Single	Co. Dub
Josephine	Donnelly	Roman Catholic	Read & write	14	Pupil	Single	
Agnes	O'Farrell	Roman Catholic	Read & write	15	Pupil	Single	Dublin
Moira	Harrington	Roman Catholic	Read and write	15	Pupil	Single	Dublin C
Stephanie	Davis	Roman Catholic	Read and write	15	Pupil	Single	Co Dub
Margret	Murray	Roman Catholic	Read and write	15	Pupil	Single	Co Wick
Anne	Dee	Roman Catholic	Read and write	14	Pupil	Single	Co. Tipper
Jane E.J.	Fox	Roman Catholic	Read and write	14	Pupil	Single	Co. Dub
Bridget	Fleming	Roman Catholic	Read and write	14	Pupil	Single	Co. Tipper
Mary Cecilia	Dwyer	Roman Catholic	Read and write	14	Pupil	Single	Co. Tipper
Bridget	Fitzgerald	Roman Catholic	Read and write	14	Pupil	Single	King's C
Bridget	Byrne	Roman Catholic	Read and write	14	Pupil	Single	Co. Wick
Florence	Duffy	Roman Catholic	Read and write	14	Pupil	Single	Dublin

Census Dublin 1911, Castleknock Townland, 24/6/1, Forms A & G40